# Sonoma County Bike Trails

*Revised Edition*

*Easy to Challenging Bicycle Rides
for Touring and Mountain Bikes*

by
**Phyllis L. Neumann**
**Author of *Marin County Bike Trails***

**Illustrations by Mary H. Dicke**

PENNGROVE PUBLICATIONS
50 Crest Way
Penngrove, CA 94951
(707) 795-8911

*To Bob, Cindy, and Andrea,*
*whose encouragement and support*
*made this book possible.*

"I would rather be ashes than dust!" by Jack London
Reprinted by permission of Milo Shepard, executor of the Jack London estate.

"Grapes" by Alexander Pushkin
From THE POEMS AND PROSE OF PUSHKIN, edited by Avrahm Yarmolinsky. Copyright 1936 and renewed 1964 by Random House, Inc. Reprinted by permission of Random House, Inc.

"Once by the Pacific" and "The Road Not Taken" by Robert Frost
From THE POETRY OF ROBERT FROST, edited by Edward Connery Lathem. Copyright 1916, 1928 © 1969 by Holt, Rinehart and Winston. Copyright 1944, © 1956 by Robert Frost. Reprinted by permission of Holt, Rinehart and Winston, Publishers.

"Pastoral" by Edna St. Vincent Millay
From COLLECTED POEMS, Harper & Row. Copyright 1921, 1948 by Edna St. Vincent Millay.

---

Printed in the United States of America by:
Lithocraft, Inc., 947 Piner Place, Santa Rosa, California

First printing, February 1978
Eighth printing, May 1988
Second edition, June 1989

*Cover photography by Jeff Dooley*
*Photo taken looking northeast on Red Winery Road in Geyserville*
*Cyclists: Cindy Neumann and Marshall Vincent*

PENNGROVE PUBLICATIONS
50 Crest Way
Penngrove, California 94951
(707) 795-8911

# TABLE OF CONTENTS

# ACKNOWLEDGMENTS

All books need the help of good friends and family to stimulate and encourage such a large undertaking. I could not have written this book without it. Therefore, in warmest appreciation I wish to thank:

SANDY AND LAMOYNE FRANK, who first discussed the idea with me about writing a bicycle touring book, and gave me the support and energy I needed as well as many of their own hours I extend my sincere thanks.

STEVE AND NANCY PHILLIPS. To Steve, for the generous use of his aircraft altimeter; and to Nancy, for her companionship on many of the rides and her helpful critique of the book.

JOHN AND JAN GILMAN. To John, for his help in riding and writing a couple of the trips; and to Jan, for her beautiful photographs.

TOM FOREMAN AND LOUISE COOLEY, for their time and expertise in editing the book.

BARBARA LINDE, for her tireless effort and determination in helping to get the book promoted. My sincere appreciation.

RAWLS FRAZIER, for his design and writing of the Highway 101 Access Route from Cloverdale to Petaluma. Thanks, Rawls.

A very special appreciation to my husband, BOB, for his frank and helpful criticism, his proofreading and editing, and his constant encouragement and support in working on the book, as well as his companionship on many of the rides.

A special thank you to my daughters, CINDY and ANDREA, for their forebearance and support through so many busy hours.

And to the many others whose ideas and opinions helped to make this book possible I offer my siincerest gratitude.

Photo credits are given to:
JEFF DOOLEY — cover, pages 38, 63
KAY FIELD — page 82
JAN GILMAN — pages 1, 11, 15, 26, 28, 29, 42, 51, 52, 56, 68, 71, 74, 75, 85
CINDY NEUMANN — pages 18, 22, 23, 44, 59, 60, 78, 81
PHYLLIS NEUMANN — page 12
SOUVERAIN CELLARS — page 34

## GOING DOWN HILL ON A BICYCLE

With lifted feet, hands still
I am poised, and down the hill
Dart, with heedful mind;
The air goes by in a wind.

Swifter and yet more swift,
Till the heart with a mighty lift
Makes the lungs laugh, the throat cry: —
"O bird, see; see, bird, I fly.

"Is this, is this your joy?
O bird then I, though a boy,
For a golden moment share
Your feathery life in air!"

Say, heart, is there aught like this
In a world that is full of bliss?
'Tis more than skating, bound
Steel-shod to the level ground.

Speed slackens now, I float
Awhile in my airy boat;
Till, when the wheels scarce crawl,
My feet to the treadles fall.

Alas, that the longest hill
Must end in a vale; but still,
Who climbs with toil, wheresoe'er,
Shall find wings waiting there.

—Henry Charles Beeching

## EXPLORE SONOMA COUNTY BY BIKE!

One of the best places for bicycling is *SONOMA* COUNTY, with its tranquil country roads, gently rolling farmlands, towering redwoods, lush vineyards, and breathtaking coastline. This is an ideal area for spending many glorious days on your bike, exploring the diverse regions that make this county so unique and enjoyable.

**Sonoma County** is about an hour's drive from San Francisco, 40 miles north of the Golden Gate Bridge on Highway 101. It extends inland to the town of Sonoma and westward to the coast. Its moderate climate makes bicycling enjoyable the year round, and especially pleasant during the summer months when there's absolutely no rain. Depending upon your mood, you can select a wide variety of terrain and climate for a bike trip. The coast is mountainous, fairly cool, often quite foggy and can even get a bit blustery. As you move inland toward the valleys, the cliffs give way to gently rolling hills and the weather softens and brightens into sunny blue skies with tranquil breezes and warmer temperatures. The northern area boasts of its incredible towering redwoods, famous wineries and the Russian River; while the southern area is somewhat more agricultural, known for its large dairy farms and vast orchards. No matter what region you select for your trip you can be assured of good cycling with fantastic scenery.

Being relatively new to biking, my friends and I were surprised and exhilarated by the quaint country roads we discovered only minutes from home. We felt as if we had stepped into a painting — the kind you only seem to find in jigsaw puzzles. The riding on these back roads was safe, easy, and yet exciting. We began exploring more of the county when we discovered bike racks and transported our bikes to recommended locations. Local bike enthusiasts all had their own ideas of the best bike routes to take. We tried them and incorporated many of our favorites into this book. The ones with too much traffic or too little scenery were discarded. We did include some especially beautiful, but challenging, rides for more ambitious or experienced riders. In all, there are over *450 miles* of biking trails in this book — enough to keep you on the road for quite a while!

**Sonoma County Bike Trails** has been written with the casual cyclist in mind — the person or family that wants to take advantage of the lush and varied Sonoma County countryside and to stop along the way at interesting spots for a picnic, a wine tour, some sightseeing, or just a breather. We could have used a book like this when we were getting started. We hope you can use it now!

### *HAPPY BICYCLING!*

Phyllis Neumann

1

# SOME TIPS FOR BETTER TOURING

All bicyclists have individual needs, depending upon their riding styles, degrees of experience, and personalities. A beginner cannot keep pace with an experienced cyclist, and therefore shouldn't try. He needs more frequent rest stops and gentler grades to keep him from having a miserable time, defeating the purpose of a pleasant day's outing. We learned that the hard way. We nearly burned ourselves out one day in our efforts to keep pace with an active cycling club whose typical morning warm-up rides were over 35 miles! We struggled to keep up for quite a while and were just about ready to pack it in when we decided to forget the club and take it at our own pace. We began talking to each other again, instead of frantically grinding away at the pedals; and we focused once again on the scenery, realizing that we had forgotten that it even existed. The trip took over an hour longer to complete (everyone had gone home), but it taught us a good lesson and renewed our faith in bicycling.

**How can you improve your riding efficiency?** Experienced cyclists develop a rhythm and pedal at a relatively constant rate of speed. This is called *cadence* and is measured in crank revolutions per minute (rpm). Each individual has a natural cadence which feels most comfortable for him. Casual cyclists seem to develop a cadence rate between 55-75 rpm; whereas serious cyclists establish a cadence somewhere between 100-140 rpm. Beginners often tend to pedal too slowly. Count your pedal strokes per minute. If your rate is much below 60 rpm, try pedaling faster by switching to a lower gear to maintain a good average pace.

The most common mistake beginners make is to start off with a burst of speed in the morning and then burn out before noon. It is more efficient to keep up a steady rhythm, mile after mile, uphill or down, rather than to use the "pedal-coast" style of riding. The body works best when it builds up stamina evenly and gradually instead of in short spurts, thereby tiring less quickly.

The gears on a 10-speed bicycle permit you to maintain your most efficient natural cadence, regardless of most terrain. When pedaling becomes too easy and there is little pedal resistance, shift to a higher gear; when it gets too difficult to maintain cadence, shift to a lower gear. (Of course, there are times when nothing helps. Those are the times to get off and hike it!)

**A note of interest for you calorie-counters:** Moderate cycling uses up an average of 5 calories per minute, or 300 calories per hour. Vigorous cycling, the kind you do going up a hill, uses up approximately 10 calories per minute, or 600 calories per hour. Therefore, in a 3-hour trip you can easily use up over 1,000 calories — provided that you don't stop at the nearest restaurant and gorge yourself when the ride is over! *(3500 calories = 1 pound)*

# HOW TO USE THIS BOOK

The way people take a bike trip covers a wide range of needs and speeds. This book is for people who are comfortable with rides where the looking and the touring are just as important as the pedaling. Many of the rides are around 20 miles long. There are short, easy rides for families with small children, and challenging rides for those out for a day's adventure.

Even a 20-mile ride can have varying degrees of difficulty and can be taken at a multitude of speeds. The variables seem to depend upon individual capabilities, equipment, weather conditions, terrain, or just how you feel that day and who you're with.

**THE RIDING TIME** specified in the book is to be used only as a flexible guide. It does not take into account rest stops or sightseeing. In general, you can estimate your own riding time as follows:

| | |
|---|---|
| 5 - 10 miles per hour | beginning or inexperienced riders traveling at a casual, leisurely pace. |
| 10 - 20 miles per hour | good, strong riders traveling at a moderate pace |
| 20 - 30 miles per hour | serious cyclists in good condition traveling at a steady, brisk pace |

**THE RIDES** have all been designed as loop trips, in that they end at the same place they begin without retracing their path. No pickup car is needed. They have been rated as **easy, medium,** or **challenging.**

**An easy ride** is one that is relatively short (10 miles or less), has easy or few grades, and can be ridden by beginners and children of all ages.

**A medium ride** is usually a bit longer (10-25 miles), and may include some moderate grades, though none too strenuous or too steep.

**A challenging ride** is for experienced riders (or ambitious ones). It is not geared for everyone, and will exhaust the beginner or novice rider. The grades are steep (walk-ups) and there may be several of them. These trips usually take at least half a day to complete without stops, and generally measure 20 miles or longer.

**MAPS** of the ride indicate the route to be ridden in strong, bold lines, while the adjoining roads are marked in lighter lines. Variations and extensions of the ride are indicated by broken lines. Interesting places to stop are also noted on the map, as well as nearby bike shops for repairs. The arrow shows you where to begin and in what direction.

**ELEVATION PROFILES** were taken for each trip, and were recorded at ½-mile intervals. They are invaluable in giving a picture of the terrain and will help you to determine whether the trip is more (or less) difficult than you want to tackle that day.

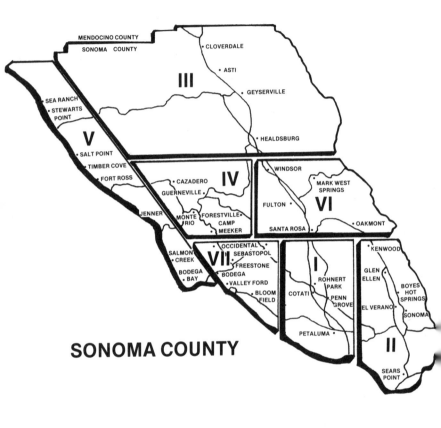

MENDOCINO COUNTY
SONOMA COUNTY

• CLOVERDALE

• ASTI

III

• GEYSERVILLE

• SEA RANCH

• STEWARTS
POINT

V

• HEALDSBURG

• SALT POINT

TIMBER COVE •

• CAZADERO

IV

• WINDSOR

• MARK WEST
SPRINGS

• FORT ROSS

GUERNEVILLE •

FULTON •

VI

JENNER

MONTE
RIO

FORESTVILLE •
CAMP
MEEKER •

SANTA ROSA •

• OAKMONT

• OCCIDENTAL
SEBASTOPOL

• KENWOOD

SALMON
CREEK

VII

FREESTONE

I

GLEN
ELLEN

BODEGA
• BAY

BODEGA
• VALLEY FORD

ROHNERT
PARK

COTATI

PENN
GROVE

EL VERANO •

BOYES
HOT
SPRINGS

• BLOOM
FIELD

• SONOMA

PETALUMA •

II

**SONOMA COUNTY**

SEARS
POINT •

4

# REGIONS OF SONOMA COUNTY

## I. SOUTHERN SONOMA COUNTY

*Beautiful agricultural setting of fertile plains and rolling hills. Famous for its poultry industry, Petaluma was once considered to be "The Egg Capital of the World." The area's large dairy farms still serve much of the bay area.*

## II. THE SONOMA VALLEY    "Valley of the Moon"

*Richly endowed with much of California's early history and magnificent old wineries. The valley's orchards, vineyards, and steaming hot springs make this area a landmark. Jack London's beautiful "Valley of the Moon" is visible from his old home in Glen Ellen.*

## III. NORTHERN SONOMA COUNTY

*The heart of wine country. Many excellent wineries surround this area, and lush fertile vineyards and orchards stretch out for miles. The beauty of the countryside is at its height in March, when prune trees are in bloom.*

## IV. THE RUSSIAN RIVER REGION

*Famous for being Sonoma County's recreational playland. Resort communities line the Russian River in a fantastic setting of redwoods, vineyards, and orchards.*

## V. THE COASTAL REGION

*Some of the most magnificent and breathtaking coastline in the world. Coastal bluffs, steep slopes giving way to fields of grazing sheep, and numerous beach coves offer majestically rugged beauty overlooking the vast Pacific Ocean.*

## VI. THE SANTA ROSA AREA

*Santa Rosa, the county seat and largest city in Sonoma County, offers some excellent bike trails within its city limits. Just outside its busy hub you will find rolling hills and a panoramic countryside.*

## VII. THE SEBASTOPOL AREA

*Nestled in beautiful rolling farmlands dotted with oak, eucalyptus, and redwood groves, as well as miles of orchards. Sebastopol is known for its Gravenstein apples. The trees are exquisite around Easter when the blossoms are at their peak, and again in August when the apples are ripe and ready for picking.*

# CALENDAR OF SONOMA COUNTY
# ANNUAL EVENTS

## JANUARY
**CLOVERDALE** Crab Cioppino Feed, Citrus Fair Pavillion (last Saturday in January), 5 p.m.

**CLOVERDALE** Fiddler's Contest, Cloverdale Fairgrounds (first weekend in January)

## FEBRUARY
**CLOVERDALE** Annual Citrus Fair and Parade, Citrus Fairgrounds (Washington's Birthday weekend, Friday through Monday), 10 a.m.

## MARCH
**HEALDSBURG** Spring Blossom Tour, Arts & Crafts Show, Villa Chanticleer on Fitch Mountain (end of March weekend)

**MONTE RIO** Annual Slugfest, North Woods Restaurant (2nd weekend in March), 1-5 p.m.

## APRIL
**BODEGA BAY** Fisherman's Festival, Boat Parade, Arts & Crafts Show (first or second weekend in April)

**SEBASTOPOL** Apple Blossom Festival and Tour, Veteran's Memorial Building (second weekend in April)

## MAY
**CLOVERDALE** Sheepdog Trials and Ram Sale, City Park (Memorial Day weekend)

**GEYSERVILLE** May Festival, Hoffman Grove (May Day weekend)

**HEALDSBURG** Future Farmers Country Fair and Parade, Recreation Park (fourth Thursday, Friday and Saturday in May)

**HEALDSBURG** Russian River Wine Festival, Healdsburg Plaza (third Sunday in May)

**PETALUMA** "Art in the Park," Walnut Park 10-5 p.m.

**PETALUMA** Butter & Egg Day Parade (first Saturday in May), 11:30 a.m.

**SANTA ROSA** "A Day Under the Oaks," Santa Rosa Junior College, open house and community fair.

**SANTA ROSA** Luther Burbank Rose Festival and Parade, downtown Santa Rosa (third weekend in May)

## JUNE
**GUERNEVILLE** Russian River Rodeo and Stumptown Days, pancake breakfast, Birkhofer Field (second week in June)

**PETALUMA** Sonoma-Marin Fair, Petaluma Fairgrounds (third week in June)

| | |
|---|---|
| *SANTA ROSA* | Artrium Arts Festival, Santa Rosa Junior College |
| *SANTA ROSA* | Arabian Horse Show, Sonoma County Fairgrounds |
| *SONOMA* | Annual Ox Roast, Sonoma Plaza (first Sunday in June) |
| *SONOMA* | Bear Flag Day Celebration, Sonoma Plaza (second Sunday in June) |
| *SONOMA* | Plaza Art Show (first weekend in June) |
| *SONOMA* | Turkey Barbecue, Sonoma Plaza (last Sunday in June) |
| *SONOMA* | Valley of the Moon Chili Cook-off, Sonoma Plaza, (second Sunday in June), 9-4:30 p.m. |
| *SONOMA* | Wine Country Roundup, Sonoma's Annual Rodeo, Maxwell Farms, Hwy. 12 (first weekend in June) |

## JULY

| | |
|---|---|
| *CLOVERDALE* | Annual Street Dance, Citrus Fairgrounds (last Saturday in July) |
| *HEALDSBURG* | Fitch Mountain Foot Race, Healdsburg Plaza (early July) |
| *KENWOOD* | Fourth of July Fireworks Celebration and Parade, downtown Kenwood |
| *MONTE RIO* | Rocky Beach Games, Monte Rio Beach (Fourth of July weekend) |
| *PENNGROVE* | Penngrove Days Parade and Barbecue, Penngrove Park (Fourth of July weekend) |
| *SANTA ROSA* | Sonoma County Fair, Sonoma Fairgrounds (last week of July, first week of August) |
| *SEBASTOPOL* | Terriyaki Barbecue, Buddhist Temple (second Sunday in July) |
| *SONOMA* | Old-Fashioned Fourth Fireworks Celebration & Parade, Sonoma Plaza |
| *SONOMA* | Pioneer Days in the Plaza (last Saturday in July) |

## AUGUST

| | |
|---|---|
| *BLOOMFIELD* | Annual Steak Barbecue, Bloomfield Park, 12-5 p.m. |
| *CLOVERDALE* | Art Festival, Italian Swiss Colony Winery (mid-August weekend) |
| *CLOVERDALE* | Wine Country Fly-In, Cloverdale Airport, pancake breakfast, helicopter rides over vineyards (end of August weekend, 9:00 a.m. |
| *COTATI* | Indian Summer Festival, Indian dancing, arts & crafts, Cotati Plaza, 11-6 p.m. |
| *PETALUMA* | Old Adobe Fiesta and Outdoor Art Show, Old Adobe Historic Park (third Sunday in August) |
| *PETALUMA* | Ugly Dog Contest, pancake breakfast, Petaluma Fairgrounds (first weekend in August), 12-3:30 p.m. |
| *SANTA ROSA* | Annual Statewide Outdoor Art Show, Veteran's Memorial Building |

| | |
|---|---|
| SANTA ROSA | California State Horsemen's Association Horse Show, Sonoma Fairgrounds (mid-two weeks in August) |
| SEBASTOPOL | Gravenstein Apple Fair, Ragle Ranch Park (second weekend in August) |

## SEPTEMBER

| | |
|---|---|
| CLOVERDALE | Cloverdale Harvest Fair, Citrus Fairgrounds (second weekend in September) |
| GUERNEVILLE | Russian River Jazz Festival, Johnson's Beach (second weekend in September) |
| PETALUMA | River Raft Regatta, Turning Basin, Petaluma River, 12-4 p.m. |
| ROHNERT PARK | Founder's Day Parade and Events, Alicia Park (second weekend in September) |
| SANTA ROSA | Scottish Gathering and Games, Sonoma County Fairgrounds (Labor Day weekend) |
| SONOMA | Valley of the Moon Vintage Festival, Sonoma Plaza (last weekend in September) |

## OCTOBER

| | |
|---|---|
| GEYSERVILLE | Fall Color Tour (last weekend in October) |
| HEALDSBURG | Healdsburg Wine Symposium, Piper Sonoma Cellars (third weekend in October) |
| PETALUMA | World Wristwrestling Championships, Petaluma Veteran's Memorial Building (2nd Saturday in October) |
| SANTA ROSA | Sonoma County Harvest Fair, Sonoma Fairgrounds (first weekend in October) |

## NOVEMBER

| | |
|---|---|
| CLOVERDALE | Christmas Faire, St. Peter's Church (third weekend in November) |
| GEYSERVILLE | Hollyberry Fair, Arts & Crafts, Souverain Winery (Thanksgiving Day weekend, Friday through Sunday) |
| HEALDSBURG | Christmas Bazaar, Healdsburg Community Center (last weekend in November) |
| ROHNERT PARK | Wine Fest, crafts, wine-tasting (second weekend in November) |
| SANTA ROSA | Christmas Craft Show, Veteran's Memorial Building |

## DECEMBER

| | |
|---|---|
| PETALUMA | Holiday Boat Parade, Petaluma River (3rd weekend in December) |
| ROHNERT PARK | Miniature Christmas Tree Festival, Community Center (first weekend in December) |
| SANTA ROSA | Holiday Crafts Fair, Community Recreation Center |

# I. SOUTHERN SONOMA COUNTY

A FARM PICTURE

Through the ample open door of the peaceful country barn,
A sunlit pasture field with cattle and horses feeding,
And haze and vista, and the far horizon fading away.

WALT WHITMAN

# 1 PETALUMA TO THE CHEESE FACTORY

**REGION:** *SOUTHERN SONOMA COUNTY*

**MILEAGE:** *21.5 MILES (3 - 4 HOURS RIDING TIME)*

**RATING:** *CHALLENGING RIDE — A scenic route along country roads with picturesque rolling hills and peaceful dairy farms. Several difficult climbs make this trip a struggle, but worth the effort.*

**ROUTE:** *Take "D" Street from Walnut Park and follow it directly to the Cheese Factory. Backtrack about a mile and turn left on Wilson-Hill Road. Turn right on Chileno Valley Road and right again on Western Avenue. This road will take you back to Petaluma. Turn right on Howard Street, left on "D" Street back to Walnut Park.*

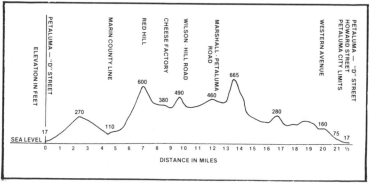

**Begin your trip** at Walnut Park, located at "D" Street in downtown Petaluma. Noted for its egg and poultry production, Petaluma has been known for years as the "World's Egg Basket." It is also a major dairy industry center and an inland port at the head of the Petaluma River, connecting Southern Sonoma County with San Francisco Bay.

"D" Street emphasizes the charm and quaintness of the town and takes you through Petaluma's most elegant neighborhood, lined with expensive vintage homes and small estates. A moderate climb marks the outskirts of the city and exposes miles of scenic dairyland punctuated by rolling hills and grazing cattle. Occasional cars and trucks use these country roads, but usually the air is filled with singing birds and gentle breezes. The several climbs begin briskly enough but only last ½ mile or so before descending. You will cross a concrete bridge marking the entrance to Marin County. A sign tells you that the road curves for 2 miles. It means just that — it feels as if it is going straight up. This is *Red Hill*. There are frequent turnouts for breathers which overlook vast valleys and old dairy farms.

10

Some 9 miles further on a white arrow appears on your right pointing the way toward *The Cheese Factory*. Just over a small hill and you are there. *The Cheese Factory* is a charming place, full of the aromas of freshly made cheeses. The quaint store offers samplings of cheeses, as well as other deli treats. Their delicious home-made buttermilk is a great thirst-quencher. You can eat lunch by a lovely pond alive with ducks and geese. A number of picnic tables are set up for the occasion. Tours of the factory are offered every 15 minutes throughout the day. The tour takes 10-15 minutes and leads you through the cool chambers where the cheeses are processed.

On your return trip, backtrack about 1 mile until you see a sign pointing the way to Petaluma, 8 miles. This road runs north and is fairly hilly. At the intersection, 2½ miles from this point, a sign warns of loose gravel. This marks an ascent that is very strenuous and steep and will poop out the most eager biker. If you look down, you can see the road you just were on — 200 feet below you. The climb is worth the struggle and sweat, for a successful ascent rewards you with a panoramic landscape that can be fully appreciated on the effortless coast down. Once you are down, look for Western Avenue, turn right and follow it back to downtown Petaluma, about 4 blocks north of "D" Street. Turn right on Howard Street to "D" Street, turn left 2 blocks to Walnut Park and your car.

*The Great Petaluma Mill*, down the street, is an interesting place to browse when you are through. It is a complex of new stores and craft shops on the Petaluma River that have been converted from an old grain mill.

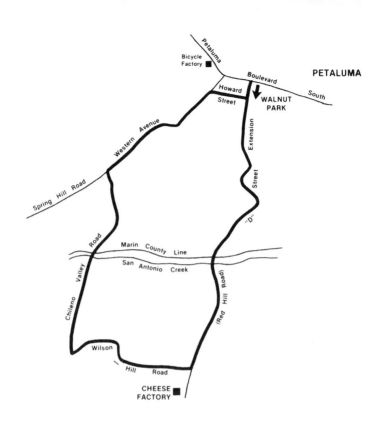

**PETALUMA**

Petaluma

Bicycle
Factory ■

Boulevard

South

Howard

Street

Walnut
Park

Western Avenue

Extension

Spring Hill Road

Street

"D"

Road

Marin   County   Line

San   Antonio   Creek

Chileno   Valley

(Red Hill Road)

Wilson

Hill   Road

**CHEESE
FACTORY** ■

# 2 COTATI TO BLOOMFIELD

**REGION:** *SOUTHERN SONOMA COUNTY*

**MILEAGE:** *24 MILES   (4 - 5 HOURS RIDING TIME)*

**RATING:** *MEDIUM DIFFICULTY — A beautiful back road ride through the heart of the Sonoma farmlands. Very light traffic and good roads make this ride relatively easy; however, several moderate climbs and a long distance might make this trip more suitable to a well-conditioned rider. The trip should be planned for the morning, as strong headwinds come up in the afternoon and you may find yourself pedaling downhill!*

**ROUTE:** *From the Cotati Plaza, take West Sierra Avenue to Stony Point Road, turn left at Stony Point and right on Roblar Road to Valley Ford Road. Take Valley Ford Road to Bloomfield Road. Turn right to Bloomfield. Return to Valley Ford Road, turn left on Walker Road to Pepper Road, which leads right to Meecham Road and then becomes Stony Point Road. Turn right on West Sierra back to the plaza.*

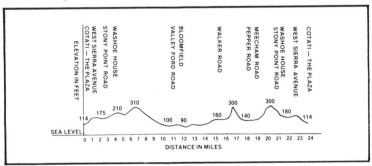

**Begin your trip** at the *Cotati Plaza,* a small and interesting place, with many of its local inhabitants being students from nearby Sonoma State University. Take West Sierra Avenue and follow it along until it passes under the freeway. This marks the entrance to the wide open country, complete with old chicken sheds, rolling farmlands and eucalyptus trees. At the stop sign turn left onto Stony Point Road. The road has a wide shoulder here for comfortable traveling. On your right you will see a breathtaking panoramic view of what I believe Sonoma County is famous for — its exquisitely rolling hills and tranquil dairy farms.

*Washoe House* is on your right, at the corner of Stony Point and Roblar Roads. It is the oldest roadhouse in California, built in 1859, and is still operating as a tavern and restaurant (a meal you may consider on the way back. I hear the food is superb.)

Take Roblar Road and view the scenery on your left. At Petersen Road you may want to take a side trip and tour *Petersen's Dairy*, or buy pumpkins or apples in the Fall. Backtrack to Roblar Road and continue on. At Valley Ford Road turn right and continue on until you reach Bloomfield Road. A sign on your left indicating *Stormy's Tavern* lets you know you've reached "downtown" *Bloomfield* (actually three streets and a fire house). On your left, before you reach Stormy's, is a wooden sign acknowledging *Emma Herbert Memorial Park*. Here you will find picnic tables, barbecue pit, and restrooms. If Stormy's is open you can pick up sandwiches, or just use the park for a quiet picnic lunch.

Return to Valley Ford Road and turn left. You will pass St. Anthony's Farms on your right, which is a church-operated dairy run by the Franciscan Fathers and part of Saint Anthony's Dining Room located in San Francisco. It offers temporary residence to 40 men until they are back on their feet again.

Turn left on Walker Road for a backroad ride to Pepper Road. Follow Pepper Road to Meecham Road and turn left. Meecham will bring you back to Stony Point Road. Turn left on Stony Point (now is the time to consider eating at the Washoe House) and then right on West Sierra, back to the Cotati Plaza and your car.

**VARIATION:** Instead of turning left on Walker Road, continue on Valley Ford Road where you will pass *Two Rock*, the location for the U.S. Coast Guard Training Center. Turn left on Pepper Road and continue the trip as described above.

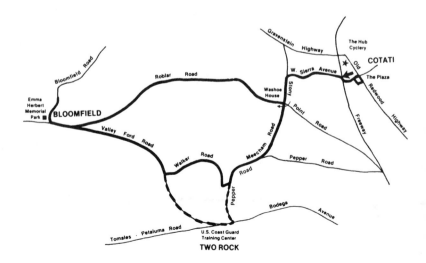

# 3 PENNGROVE AREA LOOP TRIP

**REGION:** *SOUTHERN SONOMA COUNTY*

**MILEAGE:** *10.5 MILES (1 HOUR RIDING TIME)*

**RATING:** *EASY RIDE — A short country ride through pictur-esque farmlands and gently rolling hills, with a timely pause for lunch or dinner. This is an excellent trip for a beginner or child (it was our first ride) because of its easy grades and short distance, yet it affords the experienced biker a chance to see what some of the Sonoma County back roads are all about.*

**ROUTE:** *From Penngrove Park go down Petaluma Hill Road, 1 mile; turn left at East Railroad Avenue, 4 miles, left at Stony Point Road and then right at Jewett Road. Jewett becomes Center Road, then Liberty Road. Turn left at Rainsville Road to Stony Point Road. Turn right to Old Redwood Highway. At Old Redwood Highway turn left and stay on that to Penngrove Park.*

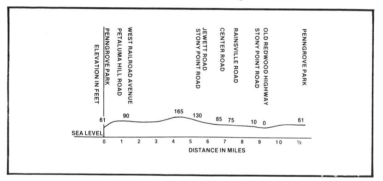

**Begin the trip** at Penngrove Park in *Penngrove,* a tiny rural community just 2 miles east of Highway 101. Penngrove was once a railroad stop, first named Penn, later Penn's Grove, and finally Penngrove. The new freeway has left Penngrove in rural peace and basically untouched.

Follow the main street, Petaluma Hill Road, through Penngrove and turn left on East Railroad Avenue. Here you will travel along peaceful country roads, passing homes with pigs, sheep, and cows in their backyards. The road will take you through attractive neighborhoods and then pass under the freeway, ending with an easy coast to Stony Point Road. Looking out from Stony Point Road is one of my favorite views — gently rolling hills, old dairies, numerous windmills that remind me of an age not yet forgotten.

Turn left on Stony Point for just a few feet and then right on Jewett Road.

Follow this winding road along scenic landscapes and tree-lined farms. Continue to Liberty Road and turn left at Rainsville Road. Enjoy a brisk coast for two or three miles until you stop again at Stony Point Road. Turn right on Stony Point to Old Redwood Highway.

The intersection of Stony Point Road and Old Redwood Highway offers the hungry biker a chance to select from no less than five restaurants of varying tastes and prices. Here is an opportunity to grab a sandwich or an ice cream cone from *Denny's*, or to treat yourself to a filling meal from *Sonoma Joe's* or *Cattlemen's Steak House*.

Complete your trip, with full tummy, along Old Redwood Highway, back to Penngrove. If there is room in your pack (or in your tummy) be sure to stop at *Palace of Fruit* for an excellent selection of fresh fruits and vegetables. If you wish to stop for a picnic lunch, *Penngrove Market* will make up delicious deli sandwiches that you can eat under shade trees of *Penngrove Park*.

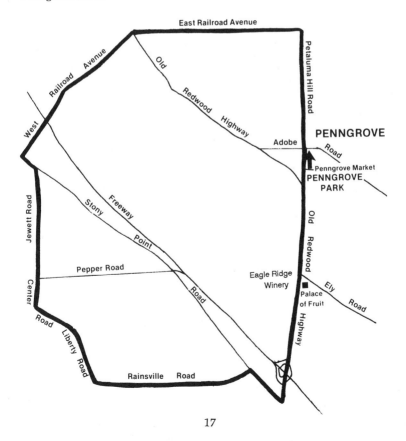

# II. THE SONOMA VALLEY "Valley of the Moon"

*I would rather be ashes than dust!*
*I would rather that my spark should*
*burn out in a brilliant blaze than it*
*should be stifled by dryrot.*

*I would rather be a superb meteor,*
*every atom of me in magnificent glow,*
*than a sleepy and permanent planet.*

*The proper function of man is to*
*live, not to exist.*

*I shall not waste my days in trying*
*to prolong them. I shall use my time.*

*JACK LONDON*

**"Wolf House"**

# 4 CITY OF SONOMA HISTORIC RAMBLE

**REGION:** *THE SONOMA VALLEY "Valley of the Moon"*

**MILEAGE:** *11 MILES (1 - 1½ HOURS RIDING TIME)*

**RATING:** *VERY EASY RIDE — Spend an entire day touring historic Sonoma, using your bicycle to take you back to the days of early California. A fun and educational trip for the whole family.*

**The first part of this tour** begins at the *Sonoma Plaza,* the largest and most interesting of its kind in California. It is the site of many festivals, parades, and historical events. The Plaza's, and Sonoma's uniqueness is that the old (for some lucky reason) was never swept away. On the north end of the Plaza you will observe building after building dating back before California became part of the United States. Some of the buildings are private and commercial in nature, such as the Salvador Vallejo Home, the Swiss Hotel, and the Blue Wing Inn.

The plaza's also a pleasant place for a picnic when your tour is over. It has grassy lawns, duck ponds, and play areas for the kids. *The Sonoma Cheese Factory,* across the street, offers local wines and other deli goodies.

The best way to explore the plaza is to leave your bikes on your car and walk casually around it, checking the quaint shops and points of interest, and filling your tummies with the goodies. Most of the historic buildings are situated at the north end of the plaza:

*THE CASA GRANDE,* built in 1836, was the first adobe home of General Vallejo while Sonoma was a Mexican town. It was later destroyed by fire in 1867. Only the Indian servants' wing remains. Entire families lived in each room.

*THE TOSCANO HOTEL,* next door, lets you view life as it was lived a hundred years ago, complete with furniture of the period.

*THE SONOMA BARRACKS,* built in 1835, of redwood timbers and adobe brick, became the headquarters of the Bear Flag Party in 1846 and was used to house Mexican army troops under General Vallejo.

*THE MISSION SAN FRANCISCO SOLANO DE SONOMA,* California's last and northernmost mission, was built in 1823, and has been completely restored. The mission was a religious and cultural center and today houses an outstanding collection of California historical artifacts and antiques. Each fall it is the scene of an authentic, colorful pageant during Sonoma's Vintage Festival.

*THE BLUE WING INN,* the area across from the Mission, was one of the oldest hotels in northern California. Now it houses antique and craft shops well worth visiting. *El Paso de Sonoma,* a complex of small craft stores and shops is in the style of a Mexican courtyard.

*THE BEAR FLAG MONUMENT,* of the short-lived California Republic, is an imposing bronze figure holding the Bear Flag. It was raised in 1846 and later destroyed in the San Francisco fire of 1906. It stands in the northeast corner of the Plaza.

**Now is the time to grab your bikes and start riding.** Take E. Spain Street past the Mission until you reach 4th Street. Here you will see that the charm of Sonoma extends well past its tourist-oriented plaza and curio shops. Dozens of turn-of-the-century houses — small, unpretentious and neat — surround you, bearing witness to the town's well kept and well-planned age. You might wonder if the street has changed at all in the last 70 years.

A left turn on 4th Street brings you to *Sebastiani Vineyards* — the location of the first vineyard planted north of San Francisco. It was first used by the mission fathers for production of sacramental wines. You can tour the mellow old stone building and investigate their well-supplied wine-tasting room. Notice the bas-relief wood carvings on the casks, doors, and walls of the winery which were done by 77-year old Earl Brown.

From Sebastiani, pedal south on 4th Street to Napa Street, turn left and follow signs to *Buena Vista Winery,* another legendary winery. Take a self-conducted tour through Buena Vista's aging cellars and wine-tasting room, built in cool limestone caverns where the temperature remains a constant 45°F. Here America's first big experimental vineyard was established in 1862 by a Hungarian nobleman, Count Agoston Haraszthy. Shaded picnic tables are placed strategically around the grounds to help you enjoy your lunch, along with a bottle of one of Buena Vista's delicious wines.

From Buena Vista return to Napa Street, turn right, then right again on 7th Street and follow signs to *Hacienda Wine Cellars.* The road is rather bumpy, but it takes you past attractive tree-lined vineyards and elegant homes. The first fine European wine grapes grown in America were planted here in 1862. There is a hospitality room and picnic area, and a beautiful wine garden which overlooks a duck pond shaded by large oak trees.

From Hacienda go straight down 7th Street, 1½ miles, to Denmark Street. Turn right on Denmark and then left on 5th Street. At Napa Road turn right to Broadway and turn right again to *Train Town.*

*Train Town*, a 10-acre railroad park, is the home of the Sonoma Gaslight Western Railroad, a scale reproduction of the 1890 period. Here you can take a 15-minute train ride behind a steam-powered locomotive.

From Train Town return to Napa Road (which becomes Leveroni Road) and turn right ½-mile to Fifth Street (just before the bridge). Turn right on Fifth, 1 mile, until you reach West Spain Street. Go half a block further to the bike path. Turn right on the bike path, which will take you right to *Vallejo's Home.*

*"LACHRYMA MONTIS," "Tear of the Mountain,"* so named because a large spring is on the site, is the Victorian home of General Vallejo, and was built in 1851. Visitors may tour both the home and storage house, which are now state museums.

Follow the bike path back to the plaza and your car. You have had a full day!

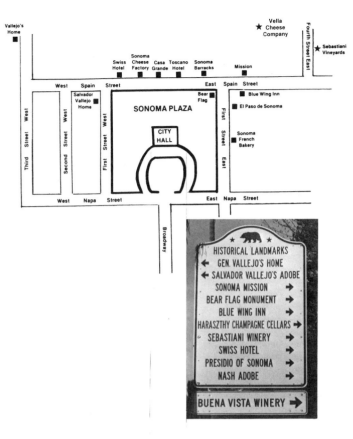

# 5 SONOMA TO GLEN ELLEN

**REGION:** *THE SONOMA VALLEY   "Valley of the Moon"*

**MILEAGE:**   *16 MILES   (2 - 3 HOURS RIDING TIME)*
*19 MILES, INCLUDING JACK LONDON STATE PARK   (3 - 4 HOURS RIDING TIME)*

**RATING:**   *MEDIUM DIFFICULTY TO GLEN ELLEN (CHALLENGING, IF YOU ADD JACK LONDON STATE PARK) The route to Glen Ellen is a relatively easy one, few hills and very scenic — a good trip for the whole family. The road to Jack London State Park is a 400-foot climb in 1½ miles. In other words, prepare to be pooped.*

**ROUTE:**   *From the Sonoma Plaza, take West Napa Street to Sonoma Highway (Highway 12); turn right. Turn left on Madrone Road to Arnold Drive. Turn right on Arnold Drive and continue until you reach Glen Ellen. If desired, follow signs to Jack London State Park. Return on Arnold Drive.*

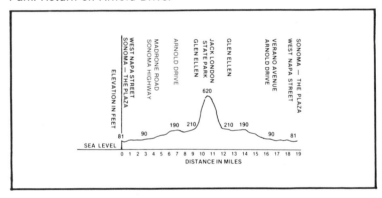

**Note:** This route has been changed because of the increasingly dangerous conditions along parts of Arnold Drive. At this time Sonoma Highway appears to be the safest route for getting to Glen Ellen. Arnold Drive, however, is more preferable for the trip back to Sonoma.

**Begin the trip** at the Sonoma Plaza. Find West Napa Street and turn right. Napa is a busy street, with fast-moving traffic, but you will not stay on it for more than a few blocks. Turn right on Sonoma Highway, which is also a busy street with fast-moving traffic, but it is also wide enough to be fairly safe and it also has a good bike lane.

Turn right on Arnold Drive, a scenic road with tree-lined homes and a lovely panorama of the hills on your right. There are broad shoulders with little traffic. You will pedal through the pleasant landscaped grounds of Sonoma State Hospital and pass over a bridge to find *London Glen Village,* a complex of boutiques and craft galleries built into an old winery. It's an interesting place to browse. For you Jack London fans, the *Jack London Bookstore,* across the road, has most of Jack London's books as well as other London memorabilia.

However you approach *Glen Ellen,* it appears rather suddenly. It hides in trees, quite literally a glen, with creeks and homes nestled in the hills. Now is the time for you to make a decision. The steep 1½-mile (the sign is inaccurate) ride up to *Jack London State Park* will poop out even the experienced biker, but you'll appreciate the lush landscaping as you walk your bike up the steeper grades. At the park, you can see the "House of Happy Walls" museum. You can walk through the quiet countryside to London's grave and view the great stone mansion, *Wolf House,* that burned down. If you've never been there it is well worth seeing. It's a pleasant place to have a picnic and relax after your trip, and you can view London's *Valley of the Moon* as well. From the park, enjoy a thrilling coast back down to Glen Ellen. Whether or not you decide to see the park, you will be returning to Sonoma via Arnold Drive.

**VARIATION #1:** Extend your trip 13 miles by riding through Glen Ellen and then turning left on Warm Springs Road, which is forested and shady. At the junction of Warm Springs and Sonoma Mountain Roads, turn right on Sonoma Mountain Road and continue on. You might consider going to *Morton's* for a refreshing swim in one of their pools, returning back to Bennett Valley Road. If not, turn left at Bennett Valley Road and continue your trip. At Enterprise Road, take a sharp left and coast most of the way back down to Sonoma Mountain Road. Turn left at Sonoma Mountain Road back to Glen Ellen. This back road ride has a beautiful country atmosphere through windy brush forest with no traffic to interfere with your viewing. Return to Sonoma on Arnold Drive.

**VARIATION #2:** When you get back to Sonoma you might want to take the *City of Sonoma Historic Ramble,* if you have energy to spare. It will add 11 miles to your trip and allow you to do some fantastic sightseeing as well.

**VARIATION #3:** Combine your trip with *Glen Ellen to Kenwood* by turning right on Warm Springs Road and returning on Sonoma Highway and then on Dunbar Road. This will extend your trip 10½ miles.

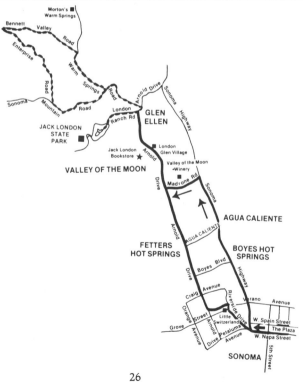

# 6   *GLEN ELLEN TO KENWOOD*

**REGION:**  *THE SONOMA VALLEY  "Valley of the Moon"*

**MILEAGE:**  *10.5 MILES  (1 - 2 HOURS RIDING TIME)*

**RATING:**  *EASY RIDE — A flat scenic tour through the Sonoma Valley on picturesque wooded back roads. A trip that the whole family can enjoy.*

**ROUTE:**  *Begin at Glen Ellen. Take Arnold Drive through town and turn left at Warm Springs Road. Follow it to Kenwood, 3 miles. Turn right on Sonoma Highway, and right on to Dunbar Road, which leads into Arnold Drive and brings you back to Glen Ellen.*

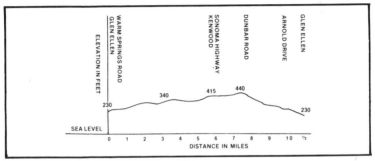

**Begin your trip** in the heart of *Glen Ellen*, Jack London's famous town. Ride through town and turn left onto Warm Springs Road. Few cars use this road and you will be immediately transported from the feeling of town to one of tranquil forest. The road gets rather winding and narrow, but the absence of cars will more than compensate.

At each fork in the road, bear to the right and the road will take you directly to *Kenwood*, a small town with a cluster of rather attractive stores that line Sonoma Highway. Across the road is the *Kenwood Winery*, which is a good place to sample the local wines. Further north on Sonoma Highway is another winery, *Chateau St. Jean*, that you may also be interested in visiting.

Turn right onto Sonoma Highway and follow it for $2^{1}/_{2}$ miles. This part of the trip is smooth with fairly wide shoulders, but there is steady traffic, so you must be careful to stay as close to the side of the road as possible. The billboard "Sebastiani Winery" brings you to Dunbar Road, which is a narrow country road, lined with vineyards and all sorts of trees and is quite peaceful compared to the bustle of the highway. Take Dunbar Road for another 2 miles until it becomes Arnold Drive. This road, wide and smooth, leads you right back to Glen Ellen.

**VARIATION #1:** If you still have energy to expend you might consider visiting *Jack London State Historic Park*. It is a 400-foot climb of 1½ miles, but the view of the *Valley of the Moon* is excellent and the museum is interesting.

**VARIATION #2:** You might wish to coordinate this trip with the *Sonoma to Glen Ellen* trip by continuing past Glen Ellen on Arnold Drive until you reach Sonoma. Return on Arnold Drive. This will add another 16 miles to your trip.

**VARIATION #3:** For the super bike enthusiast, you might wish to continue on to Ithaca, New York, as the sign indicates — *only 2,873 miles!*

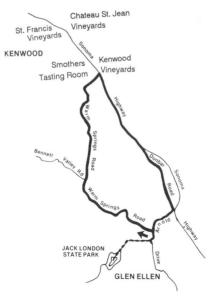

## III. NORTHERN SONOMA COUNTY

*GRAPES*

*I shall not miss the roses, fading*
*As soon as spring's fleet days are done;*
*I like the grapes whose clusters ripen*
*Upon the hillside in the sun —*
*The glory of my fertile valley,*
*They hang, each lustrous as a pearl,*
*Gold autumn's joy: oblong, transparent,*
*Like the slim fingers of a girl.*

*ALEXANDER PUSHKIN*

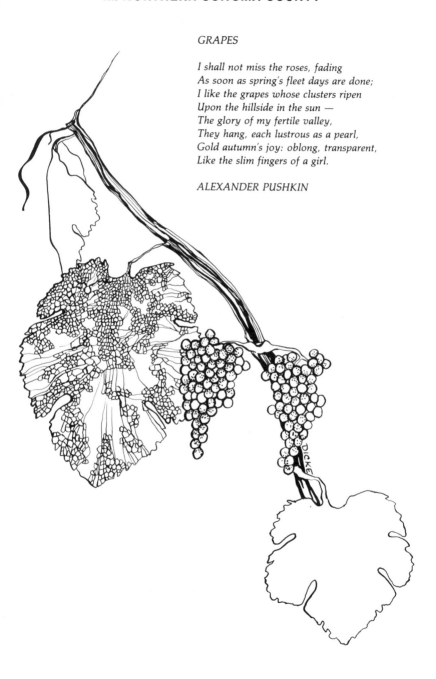

# 7  HEALDSBURG DRY CREEK VALLEY

**REGION:** *NORTHERN SONOMA COUNTY*

**MILEAGE:** *12 MILES (2 - 3 HOURS RIDING TIME)*

**RATING:** *MEDIUM DIFFICULTY — A narrow, rural valley, surrounded by lush hillsides winding through a sea of private vineyards. Easy grades and a scenic landscape make this a very pleasant trip.*

**ROUTE:** *From the plaza, take Healdsburg Avenue to Dry Creek Road. Turn left at Lambert Bridge Road and left again at West Dry Creek Road. Turn left at Westside Road back to the Plaza.*

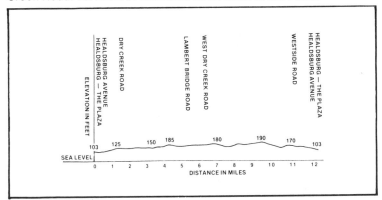

**Begin your trip** at the *Healdsburg Plaza.* Take Healdsburg Avenue north and turn left at Dry Creek Road. You will initially encounter gently rolling hills with moderate traffic until you reach a small market, *Dry Creek General Store,* at the corner of Dry Creek and Lambert Bridge Roads. This is an excellent place to stop for a brief rest on their veranda with country benches. Fill your pack with an extra snack or lunch, since they also have a small deli.

Turn up Lambert Bridge Road and be sure to stop at *Dry Creek Vineyards.* This small, friendly winery is a family operation. We always enjoy stopping here and tasting their current selection of wines, and often find ourselves returning at the end of the trip to make a purchase. They are open daily and picnic facilities are available.

From the winery, the road winds down and crosses Dry Creek at Lambert Bridge. Here the creek is quite scenic in contrast to the view closer to Healdsburg where gravel is currently being excavated.

Turn left when you reach West Dry Creek Road and you will find yourself on a quiet country road. Very few cars pass along here and the road is

31

shaded by the hillside and accented with numerous orchards. On the left you will enjoy an impressive panoramic view of Geyser Peak, Cobb Mountain, and Mount St. Helena. West Dry Creek Road ends at Westside Road and you can complete this loop by turning left and riding into the "bustling" town of *Healdsburg.* There are several small cafes and restaurants you can go to for lunch, or you can picnic under the shade trees of the plaza.

*Healdsburg* is a charming old town with an active commerical district surrounding a central plaza. During the summer you may stop at *Healdsburg Memorial Beach* for a swim in the Russian River. Facilities include bath houses, picnic-barbecue park, and a refreshment stand. The area is especially beautiful in March when prune trees are in blossom. Healdsburg is becoming the fastest growing vintage-producing area in California.

**VARIATION #1:** For an extended trip, continue up Dry Creek Road to Yoakim Bridge Road, cross Dry Creek and return south on West Dry Creek Road, meeting up with the shorter trip at Lambert Bridge Road.

**VARIATION #2:** Continue on Dry Creek Road, past Yoakim Bridge Road until you reach Warm Springs Dam. There you can take a tour of the Fish Hatchery and follow the road to the Overlook. This will give you a breathtaking view of Lake Sonoma and an expanse of the Sonoma County valley.

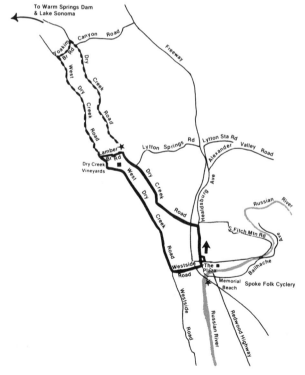

# 8 *GEYSERVILLE ALEXANDER VALLEY WINE TOUR*

**REGION:** *NORTHERN SONOMA COUNTY*

**MILEAGE:** *21.5 MILES (3 - 4 HOURS RIDING TIME)*

**RATING:** *MEDIUM DIFFICULTY — A colorful ride over relatively flat terrain, passing many interesting wineries and other attractive places to stop.*

**ROUTE:** *Begin in the center of Geyserville and turn left onto State Highway 128. Follow it as it turns right and then right again onto Alexander Valley Road. Turn right on Lytton Station Road and right again onto Lytton Springs Road. Go under the freeway and turn right on Dry Creek Road and right on Canyon Road. This will bring you back to Geyserville Avenue; turn right here to Geyserville and your car.*

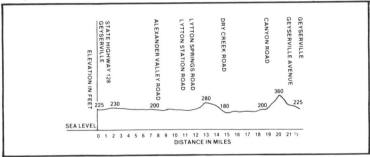

**Begin your ride** in the center of *Geyserville*, called "The Gateway to the Geysers." It takes its name from the steam geysers just a few miles to the east. Take State Highway 128 east, which is perpendicular to Geyserville Avenue. The road is flat and there are few cars. You will turn right and continue along the foothills. On the right you can see an expanse of vineyards. On the left looms Sulphur Peak, which provides comfortable shade for your ride (if you ride in the morning).

You will reach a junction where the sign tells you that *The Geysers* are only 16 miles away, a place where steam from the earth has been captured and is used to produce enough power for the needs of nearly one million people. This might be a good extension for your trip. From what I have heard, though, the road is quite steep — The Geysers are at a 2,000-foot elevation — so you decide for yourself. If not, turn right and follow the highway instead. Here the road becomes wide and smooth. You will pass vineyards all through this trip looking out over the valley. Turn right at Alexander Valley Road — the sign tells you that Healdsburg is 6 miles away. You will cross over the Russian River, a nice place to stop for a picnic or a swim before continuing on.

For those of you who wish to stay in the area for a day or so, *Alexander Valley Campground* is a nice place to stop. Continue on and turn right at Lytton Station Road. The road gets rough and narrow, the countryside becomes more barren. At the stop sign turn right onto Lytton Springs Road and continue under the freeway. Here you enter a forested area providing welcome relief on a hot day. You will pass the Salvation Army Center and begin encountering some rolling hills. Healdsburg Airport is on your left. The road narrows, but there is no traffic.

Turn right onto Dry Creek Road. The road widens to provide a good bike path and, of course, more traffic. (It seems you can't have one without the other.) Make a right on Canyon Road. This is the only really large grade you will be encountering. You will pass *Pedroncelli Winery* and later on *Geyser Peak Winery.* Both are interesting stops for sampling good local wines.

Continue on and ride under the freeway. Turn right on Geyserville Avenue, which will take you back to the heart of Geyserville and your car.

**VARIATION:** You might wish to take a short detour by turning left on Red Winery Road for a panoramic view of the Alexander Valley.

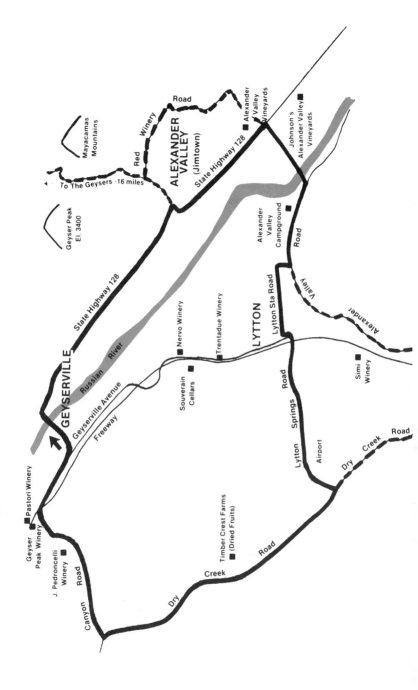

# 9 CLOVERDALE TO ASTI

## REGION: *NORTHERN SONOMA COUNTY*

**MILEAGE:** *11½ MILES (2-3 HOURS RIDING TIME)*

**RATING:** *EASY – A relatively flat ride that passes through lush vineyards and winds around the foothills and rolling countryside. This ride may not be possible during the rainy winter months because the Asti Bridge may be closed.*

**ROUTE:** *Begin on First Street in Cloverdale, which becomes Crocker Road; turn right onto River Road for about 5 miles which turns onto Washington School Road (no signs to indicate this). Turn right at Asti Road and continue to Redwood Highway. This will bring you right into Cloverdale and First Street.*

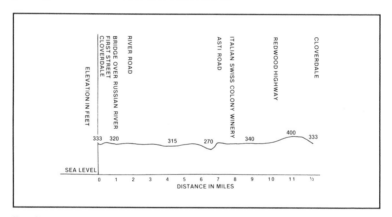

**Begin your trip** on Cloverdale Boulevard in downtown *Cloverdale*, Sonoma County's northernmost town. Its attractions include many festivals and activities throughout the year, including the annual Citrus Fair in February. Nearby are two unique churches modeled after wine vats. Cloverdale is also the northernmost spot in the United States where oranges and lemons are grown commercially.

Turn right on First Street. The road is wide with little traffic. It becomes Crocker Road and you will shortly cross a bridge over the Russian River. This may be a good place to stop and take a splash if the weather is hot. There will be another spot further along if this is too early in your ride. Crocker Road turns sharply right onto River Road. This winding road exposes the foothills on the left and lush vineyards on the right. There is no

36

bike path here, but the road is smooth with little traffic. There are hardly any grades, so relax and have a good time.

Further up a bit the road roughens and narrows as it approaches the second bridge across the Russian River. This is a good midway spot to swim and enjoy a picnic lunch. You will notice canoes passing here and local people who bring their rubber rafts. Summertime is lazy in these parts and great for splashing in the river on a hot day.

Continue your ride by turning right onto Asti Road. Be sure to check out Pat Paulsen Vineyards on your left. The tasting room occupies a colorful old wood-frame building in Paulsen's Asti Village. The Village also has shops, a tree-shaded picnic area and the Old Oak of Asti, dating back 300 years. Pat Paulsen drew media attention for years when he humorously campaigned for President. He proclaimed himself Mayor of Asti in a bipartisan ceremony on July 3, 1986.

After you have taken your fill and feel sufficiently relaxed, continue your ride (remember, you're on a bike trip) along Asti Road until it joins with Redwood Highway. At first you might think you are entering the freeway (and you will be right), but that is the only road to take and it feels less overwhelming as it becomes less of a freeway. There is a wide bike path so you are relatively safe from traffic. Redwood Highway becomes Cloverdale Boulevard and brings you safely back to First Street and your car.

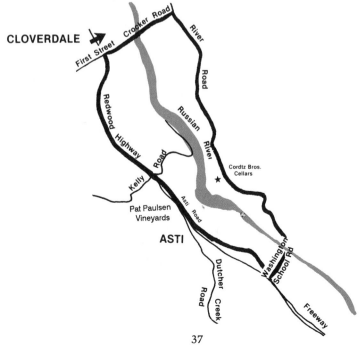

## IV. THE RUSSIAN RIVER REGION

### REDWOODS

*Older than Age itself*
  *they stand*
*And I sit silent in their shade,*
  *surrounded by these tender giants.*
*They have no match on earth*
  *yet still they strive*
*Pushing upward, ever upward*
  *against the sky.*
*With an awe that feels like loneliness*
  *though never quite alone —*
*For here, only here, is the sense*
  *of all the Universe come to*
  *make its spirit known.*

*MARYLYNNE SLAYEN*

# 10 GUERNEVILLE TO ARMSTRONG WOODS

## REGION: *THE RUSSIAN RIVER REGION*

## MILEAGE: *6½ MILES (1 HOUR RIDING TIME)*

**RATING:** *EASY RIDE — A scenic tour through the splendor and majesty of the famous California redwoods. The road to the park is wide and flat, ideal for beginning bicyclists and children. This is a great way to enjoy the Russian River Region and still have lots of time for other diversions in Guerneville, the playground of the area.*

**ROUTE:** *Armstrong Woods Road, 2 miles, to the State Park. A tour through the park, another 2 miles, and back to Guerneville.*

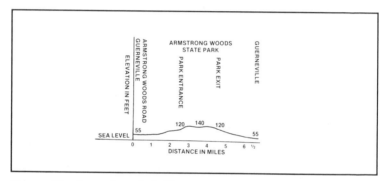

*Guerneville,* formerly called "Stumptown," was once prime redwood country. The redwoods around Guerneville were one of the grandest ever seen. Only small stands remain, such as in Armstrong Woods. The town was renamed Guerneville (Gurnville) in honor of George Emile Guerne, an enterprising Swiss who came looking for gold and ended up cutting trees instead. *Stumptown Days* is still a favorite event in June. In its honor Guerneville holds a town parade.

Resort life began here in the 1870's and flourished as vacationers came to see the wonders of the giant trees and discovered the beauty of the Russian River. Swimming, boating and water sports are popular in the summer; hiking and picnicking are big in the spring and fall; and fishermen flock here in winter when the steelhead are running. Biking naturally, is great here in any season.

**From the bustle of Guerneville,** follow the road that says Armstrong Woods Road. This will bring you right to the entrance of the park. The road leading there is wide and flat and has lots of room for bicycles. You will pass camping areas and several interesting shops along the way.

*Armstrong Redwoods State Park* contains 400 acres of natural forest growth, several picnic areas with barbecue pits, and marked hiking trails. The Forest Theater, a natural amphitheater, has a seating capacity for over 2,000 people and is often the setting for outdoor concerts (Sundays in July and August) ballet, church services and weddings. The Colonel Armstrong Tree is over 1,400 years old and climbs to 308 feet!

Bicycles are permitted in the park without fee, whereas cars have to pay. Follow the paved and shaded road through the forest. Explore the many different paths. Spend a glorious day picnicking in the cool forest, or sitting peacefully under the giant redwoods before returning back to Guerneville — and civilization. It's really a treat.

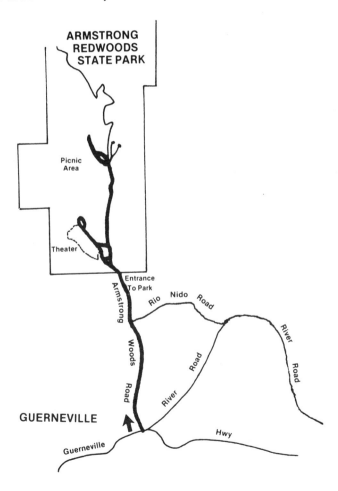

# 11  GUERNEVILLE
## River Road Ride

**REGION:** *THE RUSSIAN RIVER REGION*

**MILEAGE:** *19½ MILES   (2-3 HOURS RIDING TIME)*

**RATING:** *MEDIUM DIFFICULTY — An easy, relatively flat tour of the wooded River Road area, punctuated with cool, forested roads and vast miles of incredible vineyards. Because of the length of the ride it can be considered to be moderately difficult for some beginners or out-of-condition riders.*

**ROUTE:** *Take River Road 7 miles. After crossing the bridge turn right onto Old River Road. Turn left at Wohler Road, 3 miles, cross the bridge and turn left onto Westside Road, 4 miles, which rejoins River Road. Take that back to Guerneville.*

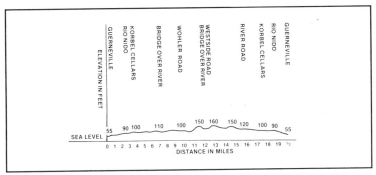

**Begin your trip** in the heart of Guerneville and take River Road towards Rio Nido. There is moderate traffic here but the road is easy to travel on. You will pass through the small but charming town of *Rio Nido,* the town "where memories linger." Just past Rio Nido, River Road suddenly illuminates a giddy expanse of vineyards and breathtaking hills. The mid-summer smells of blackberries and anise make you feel rich and alive. The road is flat and the going is easy, so this is a good time to enjoy the sights and aromas around you.

Shortly you will see signs beckoning you to *Korbel Cellars,* a winery famous for its champagne, made in the old, traditional style of winemaking. Tours that take you through the cellars and give you a step-by-step description of how wine is made are conducted every 45 minutes. A large, elegant tasting room offers you a selection of Korbel's finest wines. You will be passing by Korbel on the return trip and may find it more enjoyable then. Either time will be a treat.

River Road continues to be flat, but now becomes more forested, filled with tourist attractions and campgrounds along the Russian River where you can rent canoes. You will soon be crossing a bridge over the river, so if you have a camera handy, this is a good time to take a scenic shot.

At Wohler Road take a left. Here the road changes significantly. Traffic is infrequent and you are in the midst of orchards, vineyards, and a variety of shade trees. Wohler Road winds for a while and then joins Eastside Road at the Raford House, a bed and breakfast inn, which overlooks miles and miles of vineyards and mountains. The view is incredible. Wohler Road continues around and crosses another bridge over the Russian River. This is a good place to picnic down by the river or to take a dip. Canoes pass leisurely by, and we even saw some rubber rafts trying their luck. The river is quite shallow under the bridge and very calm, but quite barren with few trees.

Continue over the bridge and take a quick left at Westside Road. A sign tells you that Guerneville is 9 miles away. This is a beautiful road, carved through forests and vineyards. You feel as if you are far from civilization — until a car passes by. There are some easy climbs here with thrilling coasts down. Westside Road meets up with River Road to take you back to Guerneville. This side of the road, however, has uneven, rougher, and more narrow shoulders at some places, so watch out for them. The traffic speeds by pretty quickly. (Don't forget to stop by Korbel's on the way back.)

**VARIATION #1:** You might also consider combining the *Eastside, Westside Loop* to Healdsburg from Wohler Road by turning right on Eastside Road. This will add 21 miles to your trip. Return along Westside Road back to River Road, and continue as described above.

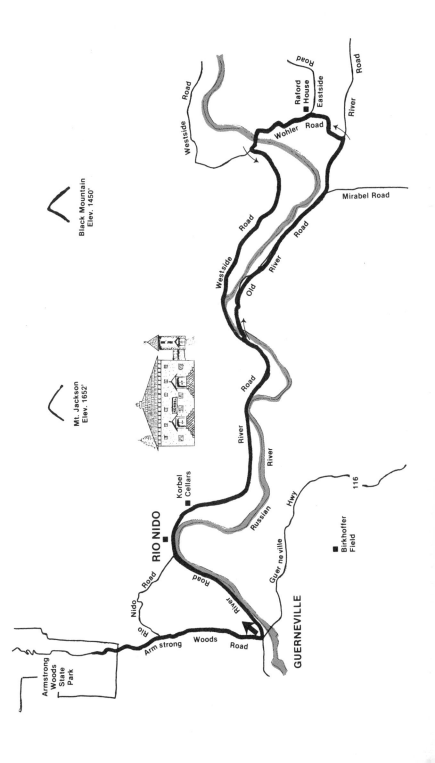

# 12 HEALDSBURG EASTSIDE, WESTSIDE LOOP

**REGION:** *THE RUSSIAN RIVER REGION*

**MILEAGE:** *21 MILES   (3 - 4 HOURS RIDING TIME)*

**RATING:** *MEDIUM DIFFICULTY — A scenic ride through forest and vineyards with beautiful panoramas of the distant mountain ranges. A basically flat road. Plan for ½-day to stop at wineries along the way and indulge in a dip in the Russian River.*

**ROUTE:** *From Healdsburg take Westside Road, 10 miles, which turns onto Wohler Road, 2 miles, and then left onto Eastside Road for 6 miles. Turn left on Redwood Highway which leads right into Healdsburg Avenue and the plaza.*

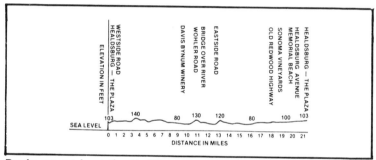

**Begin your trip** at the *Healdsburg Plaza*. For those of you who are planning a picnic lunch you might try *The Salame Tree Deli*. They make up some sumptuous sandwiches. Take Healdsburg Avenue to Mill Street and turn right. This is also the beginning of Westside Road. The road is busy and narrow and you will pass under the freeway and over what's left of Dry Creek — a gravel pit. The road now bears left and you leave the city behind and enter the quiet vineyard area. At your left you can see the mountain ranges many miles in the distance.

Westside Road is lined with oak, eucalyptus, and bay trees and the aromas accompany you almost the entire trip. The road widens now and becomes smoother where it was rather bumpy and narrow before. If you look across the vineyards you can just make out the telephone poles of Eastside Road, your route back. You pass a gravel operation which sort of puts a damper on the tranquility of the forest, after which the road twists and turns and is dotted with old farms and houses.

*Hop Kiln Winery* is at your left. They are open to the public on the weekends and, when this book was being written, was the setting for the movie, "The Magic of Lassie". Further on you will pass *Davis Bynum Winery*.

46

They have a small tasting area and delicious selection of wines that they will let you sample. The road becomes more densely wooded now and feels deliciously cool on a hot day.

Westside Road now turns right and takes you 9 miles into Guerneville. You may choose to take this road and return 17 miles later to complete the trip. If not, continue on Wohler Road, across the concrete bridge, and go for a short dip in the river. This may be a good spot to stop for lunch if you can find a shaded spot. It's rather barren along here.

Continue along this road and, at the crossroads at *The Raford House,* bear left onto Eastside Road. This road is similar to Westside Road, perhaps a bit flatter and more wooded. It will continue for quite a while. After you pass Kaiser Gravel Operations you will begin to notice colorful gravel trucks roaring by at express train speeds. They are large trucks and pass very close to the side of the road, so be careful! On your left lush valleys harboring miles of vineyards nestle below expansive panoramas of the surrounding hills. You can find Westside Road by looking for the telephone poles directly across the vineyards. After you pass West Windsor River Road you can kiss the gravel trucks good-bye. The road becomes smoother now and widens out.

At the stop sign turn left on Old Redwood Highway to Healdsburg. Shortly you will see *Sonoma Vineyards,* a modern and elegant building with picturesque pools and beautiful architecture. They have a large tasting room and you can sit at wooden tables while partaking of their large selection of wines. The staff will be pleased to answer any of your questions about wines.

Continue on Old Redwood Highway. You will be getting into heavier traffic as you approach the outskirts of Healdsburg. Pass under the freeway and you are on Healdsburg Avenue. Just before you get to the bridge you will see a sign saying *Healdsburg Memorial Beach.* This is a free beach where you can rent canoes. You might consider stopping here for a while to cool off and relax from your ride. You don't have far to go now.Once you've crossed the bridge you're practically there. The road will lead you directly to the plaza and your car.

**VARIATION:** You may want to extend your trip 17 miles by combining the *River Road Ride* and taking Westside Road straight to Guerneville, returning along River Road. This would comprise a 38-mile trip.

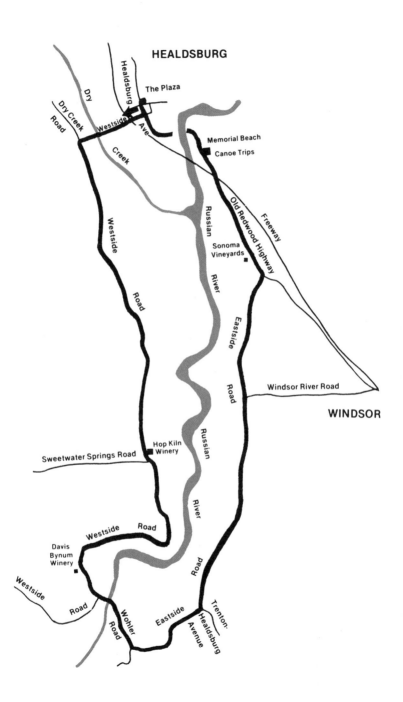

HEALDSBURG

The Plaza

Healdsburg Ave.

Dry

Dry Creek

Road

Westside

Creek

Memorial Beach
Canoe Trips

Westside

Russian

Old Redwood Highway

Freeway

Road

Sonoma
Vineyards

River

Eastside

Road

Windsor River Road

WINDSOR

Hop Kiln
Winery

Russian

Sweetwater Springs Road

Westside     Road

Davis
Bynum
Winery

Westside

River

Road

Road

Wohler
Road

Eastside     Avenue

Trenton-
Healdsburg

# 13 *MONTE RIO TO CAZADERO*

**REGION:** *THE RUSSIAN RIVER REGION*

**MILEAGE:** *20.5 MILES    (2 - 3 HOURS RIDING TIME)*

**RATING:** *MEDIUM DIFFICULTY — Take a breathtaking trip through the tall, cool redwoods, along the picturesque waters of the Russian River and Austin Creek. Here the North Pacific Coast Railroad's narrow gauge line brought sightseers and vacationers from San Francisco to the "country" from the 1880's to the 1930's.*

**ROUTE:** *Take River Road west, 3 miles, to Austin Creek Road; Austin Creek Road north, 6 miles to Kramer Road; right on Kramer Road to Cazadero Highway; left on Cazadero Highway, ½-mile to Cazadero. Return on Cazadero Highway, 6 miles, to River Road; right on River Road, 1 mile, to Duncans Mills; left across Russian River and onto Moscow Road, back to Monte Rio, 3½-miles; left across Russian River on Main Street to your car.*

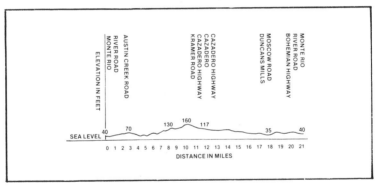

**Begin your trip** at the Rio Theater, on River Road in *Monte Rio,* carefully dividing your attention between the cars on one side and the redwoods on the other. After a brief winding narrow stretch the road widens and you'll soon make a right turn on Austin Creek Road where minimal traffic and the narrow road through dense groves of redwoods will make you feel like you are on a forest path. The gravel operation detracts from the view as you negotiate this part of the trip but helps keep the mouth of the creek open and supplies gravel and sand for roads, septic systems, and ready-mix concrete.

As the road crosses the creek and Cazadero Highway, be sure to stay on Austin Creek Road as it climbs above the Berkeley Music Camp. After passing St. Elmo Creek and a pair of one-lane bridges, turn right down Kramer Road and left on Cazadero Highway. The metropolis of *Cazadero* awaits you, sometimes called the "Heart of the Redwoods." The tiny town,

49

once a logging community, has the *Cazadero General Store* and the *Cazadero Inn* as its central features. We stopped for lunch here where the food and service are good and the bathroom is a special treat. Cazadero is also the site of outdoor concerts which are staged in the *Cazadero Music Camp Redwood Grove.* It's easy to see why so many religious and civic groups have chosen this area for camp sites.

On your return trip you will find a nice mild coast back to River Road along Cazadero Highway. You can decide to return to Monte Rio by turning left onto River Road or continue on to *Duncans Mills,* our next point of interest. This was the site of one of the many now long-gone lumber mills of this area, and now is home for a small rebuilt town with interesting shops. If it's steelhead season, you may want to try a few casts in the river just a few yards from the town, where Freezeout Pool and Brown's Pool have been popular spots for years. You might also enjoy grabbing a picnic lunch and sitting down by the river.

To return to your car, cross the river and follow Moscow Road to the left. Stay on it until you reach Monte Rio. Back in Monte Rio there are a number of spots for snacks and several excellent restaurants for dinner in this area. If you finish your trip on a warm summer's day, a swim in the river from the public beach behind the theater will be just what you need before your journey home.

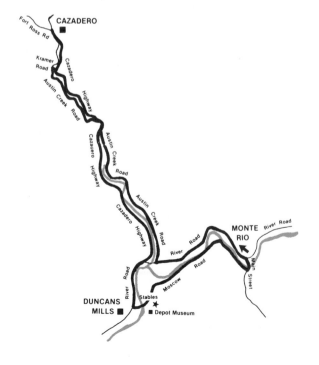

## V. THE COASTAL REGION

*ONCE BY THE PACIFIC*

*The shattered water made a misty din.*
*Great waves looked over others coming in,*
*And thought of doing something to the shore*
*That water never did to land before.*
*The clouds were low and hairy in the skies,*
*Like locks blown forward in the gleam of eyes.*
*You could not tell, and yet it looked as if*
*The shore was lucky in being backed by cliff,*
*The cliff in being backed by continent;*
*It looked as if a night of dark intent*
*Was coming, and not only a night, an age.*
*Someone had better be prepared for rage.*
*There would be more than ocean-water broken*
*Before God's last "Put Out the Light" was spoken.*

*ROBERT FROST*

# 14 *BODEGA TO BODEGA HEAD*

**REGION:** *THE COASTAL REGION*

**MILEAGE:** *20 MILES   (4 - 5 HOURS RIDING TIME)*

**RATING:** *CHALLENGING RIDE — Breathtaking coastal panoramas along winding mountain ridges make this ride a must. The initial 500-foot steep grade makes it difficult going for the average cyclist. Prepare yourself for fantastic views and a good night's sleep. An excellent trip for a picnic lunch at a scenic beach cove.*

**ROUTE:** *From the town of Bodega take Bodega Highway to Bay Highway. Turn right for 1 mile and right again on Bay Hill Road for 3½ miles, until you reach Shoreline Highway. Turn left for ½-mile and then right at East Shore Road. This will become Bay Flat Road. Turn right and follow it 6 miles until you turn left at Bodega Highway back to Bodega.*

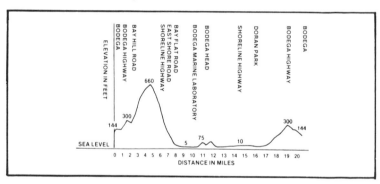

**Begin your trip** in *Bodega,* a quaint little town that was put on the map by Alfred Hitchcock's film, "The Birds." The old Potter School dates back to 1873 and is now *Bodega Gallery and Restaurant. St. Theresa's Church,* another landmark, was built in 1859. *Watson School Wayside Park* is a rest and picnic area around a one-room school house, built in 1856. There are several funky shops that make this town worth exploring.

Take Bodega Highway out of town to Bay Highway. The trip starts with a steep climb, even before you've built up any energy or developed a decent cadence. The climb is relentless and seems to continue forever. When you finally reach Bay Hill Road turn right and enter another world. You will find yourself surrounded by eucalyptus trees in a forest setting on a narrow country road. The smell of eucalyptus accompanies you on your ride. The road follows a dry creekbed on your left. Shortly the road opens up to a spectacular view of a mountain panorama with miles of barren hills. As

54

you near the top ridge you can look to your left and view the first glimpses of the coastline and *Bodega Bay*, a small fishing village. Salmon, crab, and shrimp are major industries here. During the season, as many as 500 fishing boats are busily engaged in delivering fish to the processing plants on the harbor.

Around the bend you can get a direct view of the breathtaking Pacific, as far as the eye can see. A long descent puts the ocean right in your lap as you approach the stop sign crossing Shoreline Highway. There is a lot of traffic on the weekends and it goes by pretty fast, so be careful crossing.

Turn left onto the highway and follow it ¹/₂-mile around the bend and a right onto East Shore Road. This is a beautiful flat road that follows Bodega Harbor straight out to Bodega Head, the climax of our trip and a spectacular coastal vista.

The road is wide and smooth here with a bike lane only on the left side of the road; however, there are so few cars passing that going with the traffic is no real problem. On your left you will pass a day use parking lot for boaters.

A few miles later you will pass *Bodega Bay Marine Laboratory*. This is open to visitors Fridays from 1:30-4 p.m. The road seems to end by a chainlink fence, but a sign stating "Bodega Head" indicates how to get up to the vistas. Strangely enough, there are no other signs to tell you what you will find when you get there. It was only our curiosity and adventurous spirit that made us take that steep hike in 95° weather. You will probably have to walk your bike up the hill; but persevere, for just around the bend the road levels out and you are on your way to an incredible view. If you continue straight ahead the road will take you to a dirt parking lot overlooking the Bodega Bay entrance to the Pacific. Boats follow channel markers out of the bay because of its shallow depth. A sounding buoy rings every few seconds.

The road on the right leads to the coastal vista and offers a spectacular view of the waves crashing against the rocks. There are several vantage points to this view but be careful in windy weather not to venture too far along the cliffs. Tourists have been known to have been blown into the ocean. Hikers can follow the path down to a small sheltered beach cove, or they can climb the cliffs and explore the rocks. The views are magnificent and a picnic lunch is a must for this trip.

On your return, follow Bay Flat Road back to Shoreline Highway. Turn right onto the traffic and continue along this road back to Bodega. The shoulders are good and the highway smooth, but the cars go whizzing by.

This road follows the coast for a while and then turns inland. The hills around are quite barren near the coast but become more forested inland. Turn left at the sign pointing to Bodega and follow it back to your car.

**VARIATION:** If you are looking for a short, flat but spectacular place to bike for lunch, consider just taking Bay Flat Road to Bodega Head and back. Park your car near Sonoma Dunes and plan to spend an hour or so exploring the area. This trip is only 6 miles.

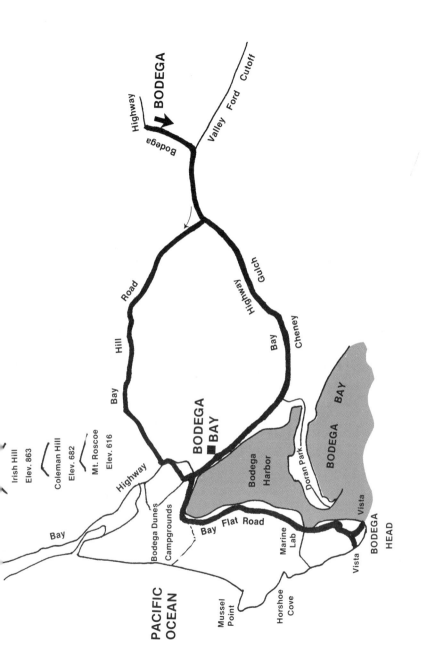

# 15 TOMALES TO VALLEY FORD

**REGION:** *THE COASTAL REGION*

**MILEAGE:** *17 MILES (3 - 4 HOURS RIDING TIME)*

**RATING:** *CHALLENGING RIDE — A spectacular ride near the coast with several fantastic views. Because of the difficult climbs in some areas, the ride may be prohibitive to beginners and children. Strong headwinds may also make this ride a strenuous one, but well worth the view if you're up to it. A morning ride when the winds are usually calmer would be more advisable.*

**ROUTE:** *Take Dillon Beach Road 2½ miles, which becomes Valley Ford-Franklin School Road at the coast, 6 miles. This road will lead you right to Valley Ford. Turn right on Valley Ford Road, past Valley Ford to Middle Road (Slaughterhouse Road) 1 mile and turn right again. At Whitaker Bluff turn left and then a quick right to an unmarked road and take that to Dillon Beach Road. Turn left to Shoreline Highway, and Tomales.*

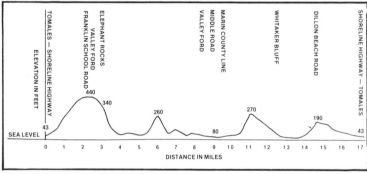

**Begin your trip** in the town of *Tomales*, a major dairy town, and take the Dillon Beach Road. This road winds through the residential outskirts of the town. Light traffic here allows you to study both the architectural design of these older Victorian-style homes and the variety of flora and fauna that surround them. Soon the road enters fertile farmlands amidst hills, bare but for brush and huge boulders sitting like sentries in the middle of nowhere.

The climb is long and tedious and will exhaust everyone but the most energetic cyclist, but the rewards are great. At the top you can see forever! An ocean panorama of extraordinary beauty discloses the entrance to *Tomales Bay* from a vast expansive sea. We happened to make the trip on a calm and exceptionally clear day. The water had not a ripple and the sky was clear blue.

At the Dillon Beach turnoff go just a few hundred feet to a vista described as *Elephant Rocks* because they do indeed look like huge gray elephants roaming the area. It is an excellent place to picnic after your long climb, or just to contemplate the beauty of the coast. A side trip to *Dillon Beach* may be desired. Be prepared for a steep descent of 400 feet and, you remember that old saying, "What goes down must now go up!" *Dillon Beach* has one or two privately owned beaches and an array of homes along small, narrow roads. If you wish to see Dillon Beach then continue down Dillon Beach Road. If not, then backtrack to Valley Ford-Franklin School Road and continue on.

This road has many spectacular views along it, but the going gets rough because the road is narrow and bumpy; however, there are few cars. A steep grade downhill can be dangerous along a winding bumpy road, so be careful! You can smell the eucalyptus groves and see cattle grazing on the relatively bare hills.

At *Valley Ford* be sure to stop at the *Valley Ford Market* and view the mural above the door. Christo's "Running Fence" put Valley Ford on the map in 1976 because the fence came right through the town, and tons of tourists flocked here for the two weeks it was up, to touch the cloth and follow it down to the coast.

Continue past Valley Ford and turn right on Middle Road, which is relatively flat compared to the road you just left. You will pass the Marin County Line and follow the road through shaded eucalyptus groves and small farms. There is a tough climb ahead, as you probably guessed. At the intersection take a quick left on Whitaker Bluff and then a right.

At the stop sign turn left onto Dillon Beach Road. This will bring you back the way you started, to the town of Tomales and your car.

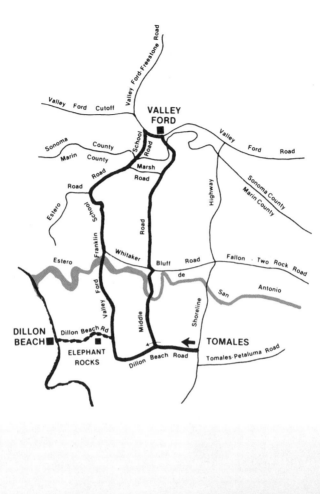

# 16 OCCIDENTAL TO THE COAST
## "The Coleman Valley Experience"

**REGION:** *THE COASTAL REGION*

**MILEAGE:** *26 MILES (5 - 6 HOURS RIDING TIME — A FULL DAY! MAY BE CONSIDERED FOR OVERNIGHT)*

**RATING:** *VERY CHALLENGING! — A spectacularly exquisite ride that soars over the coastal ranges and spans hundreds of miles of scenic beauty that touch the very heavens! The roads are especially difficult with very steep grades that will exhaust the most aggressive cyclist. Only those prepared and conditioned for such a demanding ride will really appreciate its rewards!*

**ROUTE:** *Take Coleman Valley Road, 10 miles, and follow it to the coast. Turn left on Shoreline Highway, 1½ miles; turn left on Bay Hill Road, 6 miles, and left again on Shoreline Highway. Turn left on Bodega Highway through the town of Bodega and then another left at Joy Road. Follow Joy Road, 3 miles, to Bittner Road, and then turn right, back to Occidental.*

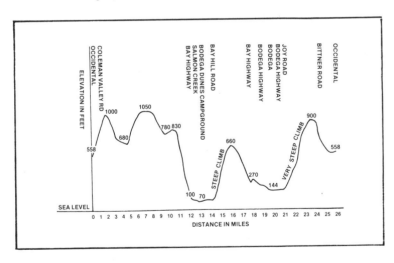

**Begin your ride** in the town of *Occidental,* a charming and colorful place. Coleman Valley Road begins right off Third Street in the center of town. The road begins to ascend almost immediately and gives you an indication of what to anticipate during the major part of this ride. It is a long, steep climb on a quiet wooded road that hopefully compensates for the exhaustion you will already be feeling. You will notice spectacular views on your right and the lush forest, as if you have ventured far from civilization. Hardly a car passes to mar the fantasy.

61

Suddenly the road opens out into a valley and then begins to climb again. Almost at the top (1,050-foot elevation) you will find a turnout (probably for overheated cars) that looks out over a vast expanse of fields and hills. The road is narrow with no shoulders, so be careful.

The road widens now and looks out over rolling meadows and vast sheep ranches. It was here that the Russians planted one of the first vineyards in the state in 1817. On a clear day you can see forever; on a foggy day you can see a few feet ahead of your nose. You will pass several cattle guards that prevent flocks of sheep from wandering too far. The weather can get quite chilly as you approach the coast; be sure to take jackets with you. Sheep can be found grazing alongside and in the middle of the road. Watch out for them.

As you get nearer the coast you can begin to see glimpses of the Pacific in the far distance. The road begins to descend rather rapidly now and gets quite winding, so brake carefully.

The descent ends at Shoreline Highway, a rather busy stretch of road (especially on weekends) that follows the coastline. Turn left here and reward yourself for your efforts with a breather on one of the turnouts. Either Coleman Beach or Salmon Creek have trails that lead down to the beaches. Here's a good place for a picnic and a dip in the ocean, if the weather permits. You might also consider camping overnight at *Bodega Dunes Campground* and returning tomorrow. If not, continue your trip by following busy Shoreline Highway for 2 miles. Turn left at Bay Hill Road. Prepare yourself for another series of steep grades with narrow winding roads and few cars. This road takes you along mountain ridges with deep, tight little valleys and quaint sheep farms. The road winds around eucalyptus groves and becomes forested and rough.

A stop sign suddenly appears at Shoreline Highway. Turn left here and proceed to the town of *Bodega.* The road is smooth here and has good shoulders as well as a few more cars, unfortunately. Turn left onto Bodega Highway which brings you right into *Bodega,* a little town nestled in farmlands with grazing cattle. It was put on the map by the movie, *The Birds.* The schoolhouse is now a bed and breakfast, but is still reminiscent of the eerie scenes in the film. Turn right on Bodega Lane to see it.

Continue through the town and turn left a mile up the road at Joy Road. The road is twisty and narrow and climbs steeply (200 feet in ½-mile to a crest of 480 feet. The road widens now and you find yourself in the midst of forest and redwoods. As you approach another major hill, and you think that you'll never get up another one again, spare yourself the agony and turn right on Bittner Road. It's a downhill coast to Occidental and becomes a two-lane road, so keep to the right. The stop sign at Scout Camp Road tells you that you have finally reached Occidental and your car.

**VARIATION:** If you want to take it a little easier on the return trip back, bypass Bay Hill Road and follow Shoreline Highway directly back to Bodega.

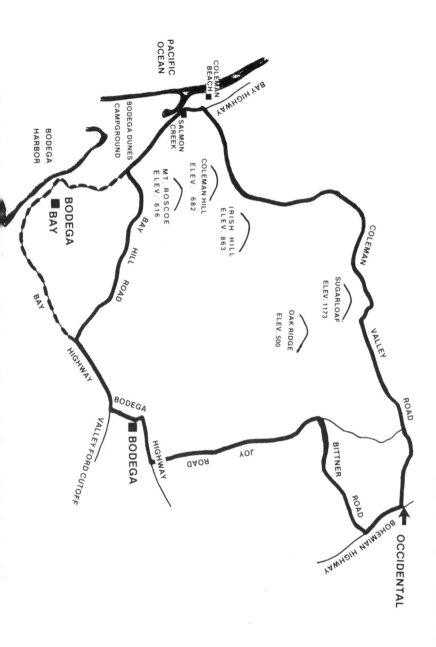

64

# VI. THE SANTA ROSA AREA

A MEMORY

*Four ducks on a pond,*
*A grass-bank beyond,*
*A blue sky of spring,*
*White clouds on the wing;*
*What a little thing*
*To remember for years —*
*To remember with tears!*

WILLIAM ALLINGHAM

**"Howarth Park"**

# 17HOWARTH PARK TO SPRING LAKE

## REGION:  *THE SANTA ROSA AREA*

**MILEAGE:**  *5 MILES  (APPROXIMATELY 1 HOUR RIDING TIME)*

**RATING:**  *EASY RIDE — Plan a fun-filled day with the entire family at Howarth or Spring Lake Parks by riding specially designated bike paths through forest woodland around Spring Lake. Then enjoy the many recreational facilities that the parks have to offer. Plan an evening barbecue or stay overnight at the campground at Spring Lake Park.*

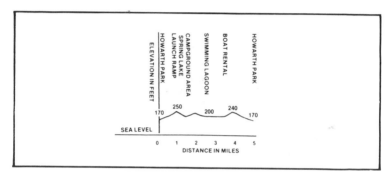

**Begin your trip** at either Howarth Park or Spring Lake Park parking area (Spring Lake will charge you $2.00 day use by car — free by bike). We started our trip at Howarth Park. A marked bicycle path specifies *Bicycles Only — No Motor Vehicles.* The path follows around the right side of Lake Ralphine and winds its way through wooded hills, leading you to the *Spring Lake Recreational Area* (approximately 1 mile). When you reach a fork in the road turn right to the campground or beyond that. Take a left at the stop sign to the boat launching ramp. The lake is used by small sailboats as well as kayaks and canoes, and sailboat races take place here often. Boats can be rented on the far side of the lake.

Continue through the wooden gates on the designated bike path around the far side of Spring Lake. Be sure to view the distant hills for a spectacular panorama of the area. The bike path brings you around the lake to the *Swimming Lagoon* area, complete with bath house, restrooms, concession stand and boat rentals.

The bike path continues from the parking lot adjacent to the boat rental and winds its way around the lake. A small climb brings you to the top of the main dam. Cross the dam for a nice downhill coast back to Howarth Park.

66

**HOWARTH PARK:** Offers lighted softball and tennis courts, picnic and barbecue facilities, hiking, biking and riding trails, and play apparatus. Big K Land offers miniature train rides, pony rides and a merry-go-round. Boating and fishing can be enjoyed on Lake Ralphine, as well as rowboat and sailboat rentals. Sailing classes are held in the summer. The animal farm, amusement park, and boat house are open during Easter vacation, on weekends, and daily during the summer months.

**SPRING LAKE PARK:** 320 acres, offers a campground, boat ramp, hiking, biking, and riding trails, picnic grounds, and a swimming lagoon. The shower rooms and concession stand are located adjacent to the swimming lagoon. The lake provides excellent facilities for small boating, fishing and picnicking. Barbecue pits and picnic tables are provided at various points around the lake.

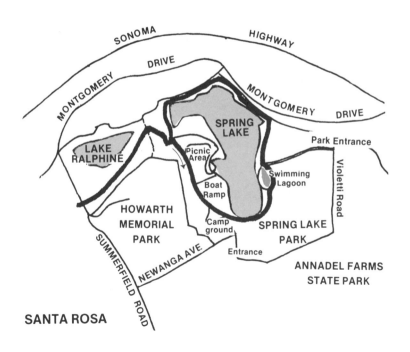

# 18 *BENNETT VALLEY LOOP TRIP*

**REGION:** *THE SANTA ROSA AREA*

**MILEAGE:** *15 MILES (2-3 HOURS RIDING TIME)*

**RATING:** *MEDIUM DIFFICULTY — A scenic ride through the Sonoma Hills along pleasant country roads. The first part of the trip includes a relatively steep grade, but the rest is comfortably level. This trip might not be suited for children due to some heavy traffic on Bennett Valley Road.*

**ROUTE:** *Take Bennett Valley Road, 5 miles; turn right on Grange Road which then turns and becomes Crane Canyon Road, 3 miles; turn right at Petaluma Hill Road, 5 miles. Turn right on Aston Avenue and then left on Brookwood Avenue back to your car.*

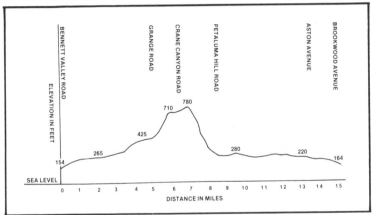

**Begin your trip** at the *Sonoma County Fairgrounds* on the corner of Bennett Valley Road and Brookwood Avenue. On Brookwood you will find ample parking for your car. Turn right on Bennett Valley Road to get out of the city. There is a bike path, but the traffic is relatively heavy for a while and, because of this, the ride is not recommended for children. As you reach the outskirts of town the road becomes forested and scenic. Traffic doesn't appear to be too heavy (we went on a Sunday) but the road winds around, making blind curves somewhat hazardous. On your left is the beautiful Santa Rosa mountain range — Sugar Loaf Ridge, Hood Mountain, and Bennett Mountain.

The road continues to wind and parallels the distant mountain ranges. You can see cattle grazing here. Turn right onto Grange Road. As soon as you turn, you are faced with an ascent through the hills. The panorama is magnificent with eucalyptus trees lining the road. Once the road becomes

69

Crane Canyon Road it indicates that you have finished your climb of 600 feet. Now it's downhill through winding tree-lined roads. Your coast ends at Petaluma Hill Road, a busier street with smooth, wide bike paths. A right turn here leads directly into Santa Rosa. As you pass the farms around this area you will notice advertising for *Crane Melons,* a delectable cross of Japanese melon that tastes like cantaloupe and honeydew combined. The melon was developed and grown exclusively in this area by Oliver Lawrence Crane in the 1930's, and the original family still lives in the area. The Crane melon is still produced locally and is ripe around the first of September.

In order to avoid the city traffic, turn right on Aston Avenue and ride on a narrow road past the rows of horse stalls of the fairgrounds. You might wish to explore the fairgrounds by bicycle. It is open to the public. You will notice the arenas, the many buildings and the racetrack. The fair is alive in July, while the rest of the year it is relatively empty with only occasional festivities and events on the weekends. The road will lead you back to Bennett Valley Road. Turn right to Brookwood Avenue and your car. If you want to bypass the fairgrounds, turn left on Brookwood Avenue and follow it directly to your car.

**VARIATION:** You might wish to extend your trip 10 miles and explore more of the Sonoma Hills by taking Bennett Valley Road past Grange Road and turning right on Sonoma Mountain Road. At the Y bear right onto Pressley Road which will take you down to Roberts Road. Turn right when you reach Petaluma Hill Road and continue the ride as described above back to Santa Rosa.

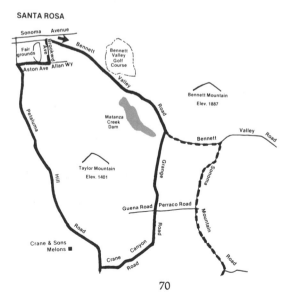

70

# 19 SANTA ROSA MARK WEST SPRINGS LOOP

**REGION:** *THE SANTA ROSA AREA*

**MILEAGE:** *15 MILES   (2 - 3 HOURS RIDING TIME)*

**RATING:** *MEDIUM DIFFICULTY — A highly scenic tour of country roads winding through picturesque vineyards and shaded orchards. Many breathtaking panoramas of the St. Helena mountain range. There is very little traffic on most roads outside the Santa Rosa city limit.*

**ROUTE:** *Take Mendocino Avenue to Old Redwood Highway and continue until you reach Mark West Springs Road. Turn right until you reach Riebli Road and turn right again. Follow Riebli Road until you turn right on Wallace Road. This will lead you into Brush Creek Road and end at Sonoma Highway. Turn right and follow Fourth Street to College Avenue. Turn right on Mendocino Avenue to Bailey Field and your car.*

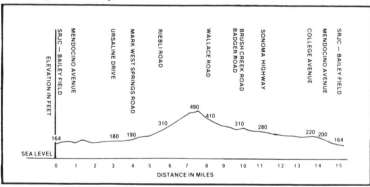

**Begin your trip** at Bailey Field parking lot at Santa Rosa Junior College on Mendocino Avenue. Cross Mendocino and proceed north out of town. Here you will be moving with heavy traffic and stop lights — and no designated bike lanes; however, the street is wide enough to accommodate both car and bike — if your luck holds out!

On your right, just beyond the busiest part of town, you will pass Fountaingrove Round Barn; on your left you will find yourself parallel to the freeway and K-Mart. Make a sharp right at the frontage road (it's not marked) and be careful not to find yourself in the middle of the freeway! Cloverleaf Ranch is on your right. When you see Orchard Inn make a right. This will put you on Ursaline Drive, a quiet, residential street. Make another right at Mark West Springs Road. Here you will find a good bike path and a long ascent to the country. Continue 1½ miles past a deer crossing sign and a billboard advertising *Petrified Forest — 9 miles.* (If you wish to make that trip, continue on Mark West Springs Road. If not, turn right at Riebli Road.)

Here our road becomes tranquil, lined with shaded oak trees and several attractive homes. Very little traffic passes by. Ahead you will find a vast panorama of the St. Helena mountain range. The road narrows here and becomes picturesquely dotted with small vineyards on the left. Watch for a curve in the road and a sign *The Foothills*, a large housing development; bear right and take a sharp climb. At the top is an open feeling of expanse. Rolling hills go on for miles. You'll make a sharp descent to a quaint farmhouse (it almost looks like the entrance to a small town, since the road runs right through the property), enjoy another panoramic view of the area, and proceed down to Wallace Road. Turn right and follow Badger onto Brush Creek Road for 3 miles. At the stop sign turn right on Sonoma Highway. And so we leave the country behind.

Sonoma Highway becomes Fourth Street, which is wide-laned and *busy!* Traffic roars by! Follow Fourth Street for 2 miles and bear right at College Avenue. Turn right again at Mendocino and continue to Bailey Field and your car.

**VARIATION:** You may be interested in taking the more ambitious trip to *The Petrified Forest* by continuing on Mark West Springs Road instead of turning on Riebli Road. This becomes Porter Creek Road and continues for 3 miles to Petrified Forest Road. Turn left for 2 miles until you reach *The Petrified Forest*. The Forest has been open to the public since 1860 and has a museum, picnic area and gift shop. It's an interesting way to spend an hour or two. For the return trip, backtrack to Porter Creek Road which becomes Calistoga Road and continue on for 7 miles, until you reach Badger Road. Turn right on Badger Road, and then left on Brush Creek Road. Continue the rest of the trip as described above.

*PASTORAL*

*If it were only still! —*
*With far away the shrill*
*Crying of a cock;*
*Or the shaken bell*
*From a cow's throat*
*Moving through the bushes;*
*Or the soft shock*
*Of wizened apples falling*
*From an old tree*
*In a forgotten orchard*
*Upon a hilly rock!*

*Oh, grey hill,*
*Where the grazing herd*
*Licks the purple blossom,*
*Crops the spiky weed!*
*Oh, stony pasture,*
*Where the tall mullein*
*Stands up so sturdy*
*On its little seed!*

*EDNA ST. VINCENT MILLAY*

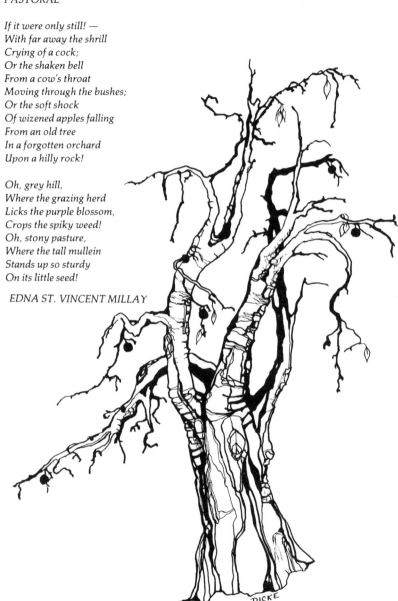

# 20 *LONE PINE ROAD LOOP TRIP*

**REGION:** *THE SEBASTOPOL AREA*

**MILEAGE:** *10 MILES (2 - 3 HOURS RIDING TIME)*

**RATING:** *MEDIUM DIFFICULTY — A relatively short trip in distance, but numerous rolling hills make the riding time considerably longer. The terrain is scenic, hilly and peaceful. A real chance to explore the back roads of Sebastopol.*

**ROUTE:** *Take Lone Pine Road to Bloomfield Road and turn left. Bloomfield Road becomes Canfield Road; bear left on Blank Road and follow it until it becomes Hessel Road. Turn left at Hessel and then right to Gravenstein Highway. Go across the highway and follow Hessel around and back to Lone Pine Road.*

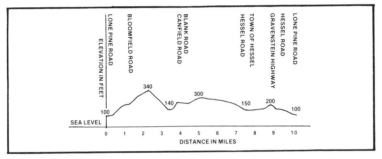

**Begin your trip,** at *Lone Pine Trading Post,* an antique shop at the corner of Lone Pine Road and Gravenstein Highway. Lone Pine Road is a quiet country road with little traffic and winding hilly terrain. The road is ideal for biking because of its smooth surface and wide shoulders, but it can pose a problem for new or out-of-conditioned bikers because of its moderately high and frequent hills. It's worth the effort though, because of the splendor of the landscape.

Turn left on Bloomfield Road and follow apple orchards down winding narrow roads. Turn left on Bloomfield again and appreciate a panoramic view of the distant hills — brown in the summer and green in the winter. You will enjoy a free-wheeling coast downhill for quite a while. Turn left on Canfield Road and left again on Blank Road. Continue on Blank Road for several miles and bear left. At the stop sign take a sharp left onto Hessel Road. This will bring you to the tiny town of *Hessel* (if you ride too fast you will miss it). At the stop sign turn right on Hessel Road. This will take you to Gravenstein Highway. You can either turn left on Gravenstein to Lone Pine Road or go across Gravenstein on Hessel, which is just a small road, but one that will give you a beautiful panorama of the distant hills and then bring you back to Lone Pine Road and your car.

**VARIATION:** Expand your trip by turning right on Bloomfield Road to the town of *Bloomfield* and returning on Roblar Road. Turn left on Petersen Road until you reach Hessel Road. Turn right and continue up Hessel as in the previous trip.

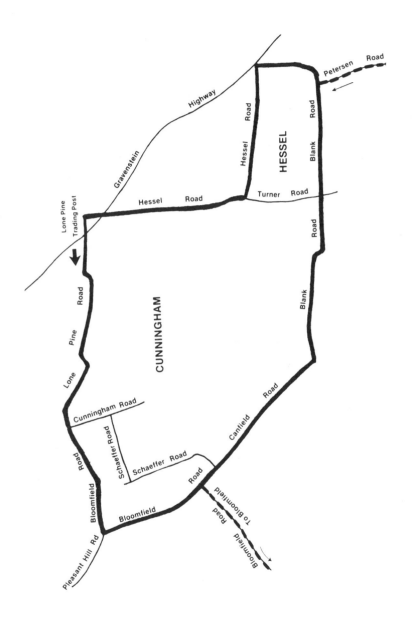

# 21 FREESTONE — VALLEY FORD BLOOMFIELD TRIANGLE

**REGION:** *THE SEBASTOPOL AREA*

**MILEAGE:** *21.5 MILES (3 - 4 HOURS RIDING TIME)*

**RATING:** *CHALLENGING RIDE — A scenic ride through hills and valleys. Several moderate climbs and fairly long distance might become somewhat strenuous and therefore more suitable for experienced riders.*

**ROUTE:** *Take Bohemian Highway to Bodega Highway, left on Valley Ford-Freestone Road to the town of Valley Ford. Continue on Valley Ford Road, 6 miles, to Bloomfield Road. Turn left, 4 miles, and turn left at Blucher Valley Road. Turn left on Kennedy Road, right on Thorn Road, and left on Barnett Valley Road. Turn left on Bodega Highway and right on Bohemian Highway back to Freestone.*

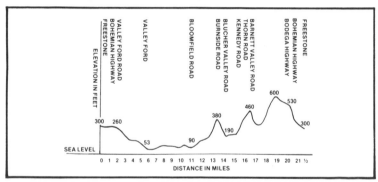

**Begin your trip** in *Freestone*, a village that got its name from the nearby quarry in 1880. The country store can supply you with picnic supplies for the rugged trip ahead. Wandering through the town is quite interesting. There are antique stores and museums, all nicely renovated and neat.

Take the main street, Bohemian Highway, back to Bodega Highway. It has good shoulders, and the road is wide and smooth. This will take you right to Valley Ford. As you approach the town the road gets a bit rougher and narrower with no shoulders, and landscape becomes quite barren with few trees. Then suddenly, the view expands into lush green (brown in summer).

*Valley Ford* is another tiny village with a modern bank and general store, and was also the central location for Christo's "Running Fence," which traveled right through the town in 1976 and attracted visitors from miles around who followed the fence to the Pacific. Over the store is a mural of the fence.

Continue on Valley Ford Road to get to Bloomfield. After the road passes Shoreline Highway it seems to smooth out and become more agricultural, passing large dairy farms. The aroma of eucalyptus trees gives the area a delicious flavor. At Bloomfield Road turn left. You immediately find yourself in downtown *Bloomfield*. Old buildings, mostly abandoned now, line the left side of the road while grazing cattle line the other. At *Emma Herbert Memorial Park* you can treat yourself to a picnic lunch and use the available restrooms.

As soon as you leave Bloomfield you begin your ascent through the hills. Eucalyptus trees line the road giving off a fragrant aroma, and provide shade for a hot and perhaps tired cyclist. At Burnside Road you can decide if you want to tackle a strenuous 500-foot climb in 2 miles for a fantastic two-sided view of the entire Sebastopol Valley, or continue on along Bloomfield Road until you reach Blucher Valley Road. Turn left onto a narrow road lined with funky cabin-style homes. The road twists and narrows but no cars pass along here. A rather tall, imposing hill looms ahead of you and you will notice large apple orchards. You can get a good view of the whole valley on your right (though I must admit not as spectacular as on Burnside Road). On a clear day the view extends for many miles and you can see the St. Helena mountain range.

When you reach Barnett Valley Road turn left. The road becomes forested and pretty as you approach a rather steep descent and wind down the mountains. Don't let the bike get away from you. Another scenic panorama of the whole valley unfolds at the top of another grade. It's really beautiful up there.

Most of the way back to Freestone is downhill. As you leave beautiful Barnett Valley Road and turn left on busy Bodega Highway you will truly appreciate the beauty of the area. A right turn on Bohemian Highway will lead you back to Freestone and your car.

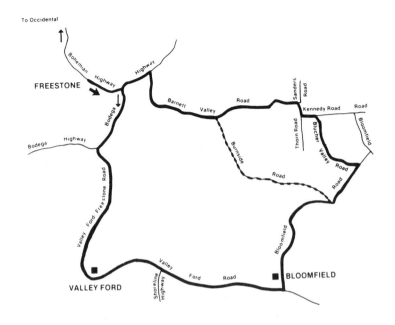

# 22 *OCCIDENTAL TO FREESTONE*

**REGION:** *THE SEBASTOPOL AREA*

**MILEAGE:** *9 MILES (1 - 2 HOURS RIDING TIME)*

**RATING:** *MEDIUM DIFFICULTY — A relatively short trip through forested roads that can get rather steep at times. Some climbs are difficult, though the scenery is rewarding. A short but rugged ride.*

**ROUTE:** *From Bohemian Highway in Occidental turn right on Occidental Road at the north end of town, 2 miles. Turn right on Jonive Road and take that for 2 miles more until you reach Bodega Highway. Turn right and then right again on Bohemian Highway through Freestone. Continue on Bohemian Highway back to Occidental.*

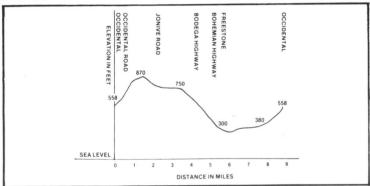

**Begin your trip** in *Occidental*, a great place to begin and end a trip because of its interesting shops and world-famous restaurants. Park your car anywhere in town and ride to the north end where you will find Occidental Road. It immediately begins to climb out of town, and the traffic tends to get heavy at times. This trip might best be planned for a weekday because Occidental is a favorite tourist attraction on the weekends. The road is smooth with an interesting feeling of wilderness, yet it is narrow with no place for bikes. The sign tells you that the next two miles are steep and winding. It is correct.

Turn right at Jonive Road and enter a quiet, forested narrow back road lined with homes and no traffic. The road peaks out after a while, and then it is downhill all the way to Freestone. That will give you quite a breather and a chance to take in the beautiful scenery. Some of the more impressive panoramas can be caught by peeking through fences of homes that have already staked their claim to the view.

Bodega Highway is up ahead. Turn right and then right again on Bohemian Highway, which passes through *Freestone*, a rather quaint small town lined with several antique shops and a country store.

Your trip back to Occidental is quite peaceful and shaded with only one mild climb on the entire road. It is forested with redwoods and there is a feeling of denseness, as though civilization has simply vanished. I really enjoy the smells and sounds of this area. Suddenly the road opens up and Occidental comes out of nowhere to greet you. Since the trip was so short, spend the rest of the day taking in the sights as a tourist and find out what makes Occidental so unique. Be sure to dine at one of the excellent Italian restaurants that boast of incredible amounts of delicious food — *The Union Hotel, Negri's,* and *Fiori's.*

**VARIATION:** If you wish to plan a more extended 25-mile trip, take Graton Road out of Occidental and follow it to Mills Station Road. Turn right and then right on Ragle Road. Turn left onto Pleasant Hill Road until you reach Kennedy Road. Turn right on Kennedy Road, right on Thorn Road and left on Barnett Valley Road. When this reaches Bodega Highway cross it to Jonive Road and take that to Occidental Road. Turn left on Occidental Road back to Occidental.

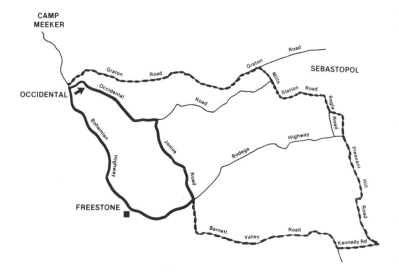

# MOUNTAIN BIKES

In the past few years mountain (off-road) bikes have captured the bicycle industry. Although 10-speed bikes are better designed for greater speed on paved roads, off-road cyclists are enjoying mountain bikes everywhere, including city streets. When using the Sonoma County Park System it is important to know the park regulations for bicycles. Check with a ranger regarding the current status.

State and county parks are the best places to ride mountain bikes in Sonoma County. Among them are:

**Annadel State Park** — in Santa Rosa, is the favorite place for mountain bike riding in Sonoma County, with its 40 miles of dirt trails and panoramic landscape (see following page). *INTERMEDIATE to CHALLENGING*

**Austin Creek State Recreation Area** — in Guerneville, has 20 miles of very steep trails. There are several different trails approximately 4-12 miles in length. There is no water, so bring your own. Austin Creek is located within Armstrong Redwoods State Park. *CHALLENGING*

**Jack London State Park** — in Glen Ellen, has about 25 miles of trails that are available to mountain bikes. There is a 10.6-mile loop. One trail leads to a lake approximately one mile from the parking lot. The only drinking water is in the picnic area. There is a $3.00 day use fee for parking. The trails go up the east side of Sonoma Mountain and are very steep. There are several vista point with picnic areas. A large fire road leads to the back country. *CHALLENGING*

**Lake Sonoma Recreation Area** — 11 miles NW of Healdsburg, has a steep 4 to 5-mile loop on a wide fire road which rides along the ridge top and overlooks the Warm Springs arm of Lake Sonoma. There are two primitive camp areas, Bummer Peak Camp and Lone Pine Camp. A camping permit is required. There is no fee. Bring your own drinking water. Trail maps are available at Visitors Center. During adverse weather conditions this trail is closed to bikes. *CHALLENGING*

**Sonoma Valley Regional Park** — in Glen Ellen, has a 1¼-mile trail with hiking and picnic area. The off-road loop has a slight hill and joins the paved walking path. There is a $1.00 parking fee. The park is located next to Glen Ellen Forestry Station on Highway 12. *EASY*

**Sugar Loaf Ridge State Park** — in Kenwood, has approximately 25 miles of trails that are open to bicycles. Most of the trails form loops, although some dead-end. As a whole they are rather steep, with some grades as much as 20 percent. Many of the trails may be unsuitable for winter usage. The park gets very hot in the summer. *CHALLENGING*

# 23 *ANNADEL STATE PARK*

## REGION: THE SANTA ROSA AREA

**ROUTE:** *INTERMEDIATE RIDE (6½ miles) — A gentle ride to Lake Ilsanjo with a fantastic panorama overlooking the lake and park. Begin at the parking lot on Channel Drive. Take Lake Trail to Lake Ilsanjo. Follow it around the lake, taking Live Oak Trail back to Louis Trail and finishing on Lake Trail back to the parking lot.*

*CHALLENGING RIDE (14 miles) — A ride to Ledson Marsh for a picturesque look at the park's wildlife. Begin at the parking lot on Channel Drive, take Lake Trail to South Burma Trail. Take a left on Marsh Trail and follow it around Ledson Marsh as it becomes Ridge Trail. Return on Marsh Trail and stay on it for a while. Bear right to Canyon Trail, left on Live Oak to Louis Trail, returning on Lake Trail to the parking lot.*

**Annadel State Park,** located on the eastern edge of Santa Rosa, has been a favorite area for off-road cyclists. Annadel offers excellent opportunities for off-road cycling with its 5,000 acres of hills, streams, woodlands and meadows. There are 40 miles of hiking, horseback and cycling trails in the park that are closed to cars. Elevations in the park range from 360 to 1880 feet, but most of the trails rise and fall gradually.

Lake Ilsanjo, a 2½-mile ride from the parking lot, is a popular destination for bicycles and hikers as well. The lake's Spanish-sounding name is actually derived from the combined first names of the property's former owners, Ilsa and Joe. Restrooms are located along the shoreline near the lake and picnic areas.

Ledson Marsh, also a popular destination, is an ideal area for observing and photographing the park's wildlife, which include over 130 species of birds, as well as deer, fox, raccoon, muskrat, skunk, bobcat and wild pig.

Drinking water is available only at the park office; carry a canteen on your bike, as the spring water is unsafe. There are a few rattlesnakes, so be alert for them as well as for poison oak. Check the signposts to be sure you're taking the trail you intended to take. Camping in the park is not permitted. Fires, camp stoves, and barbecues are also restricted. Because of the high fire hazard, smoking is permitted only in designated areas. Garbage cans are located at various points along the trails.

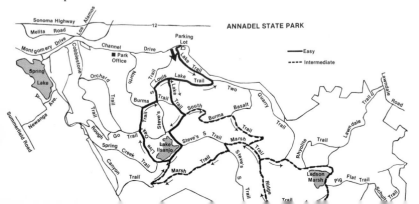

# HIGHWAY 101 ACCESS ROUTE
## Cloverdale to Petaluma

**REGION:** *NORTHERN SONOMA COUNTY*

**MILEAGE:** *62 MILES ONE WAY   (5-6 HOURS RIDING TIME)*

**RATING:** *CHALLENGING — This ride is included in the book as an access route for those needing to travel through Sonoma County as part of a tour or as a way of going from one town to another. It is not intended so much as a pleasure ride, but rather as a means to an end.*

*The route described is from north to south, roughly paralleling Highway 101. It begins in the town of Cloverdale and ends at Walnut Park in downtown Petaluma. (Note: If you are planning to travel further south please consult Marin County Bike Trails for a route from Petaluma to the Golden Gate Bridge.)*

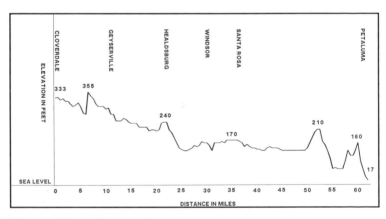

## Cloverdale to Geyserville

Begin your trip in downtown Cloverdale, Sonoma County's northernmost town. Take First Street east, which becomes Crocker Road. Cross the bridge over the Russian River and make a sharp right onto River Road for about 5 miles. You will cross a second bridge over the Russian River. This bridge, however, may be closed during winter months due to heavy rain. This road becomes Washington School Road (no signs to indicate this). As an alternate route in winter months take Redwood Highway south to just a little beyond Kelly Road. On your left take Asti Road as Highway 101 becomes a freeway.

Turn left onto Asti Road and continue on this road to Geyserville. This road parallels the freeway and is smooth and wide with no bike lane and no traffic. You will pass beautiful vineyards and orchards along the way. At the stop sign continue straight to Geyserville.

## Geyserville to Healdsburg

In the center of town turn left onto State Highway 128. This is a two-lane country road. You will once again cross the Russian River. Follow it as it winds through lush vineyards. Turn right on River Road (which is still Highway 128) and continue to Alexander Valley (Jimtown). This road also travels smoothly through vineyards on your right and Sulphur Peak on your left.

At the intersection turn right onto Alexander Valley Road where you will again cross the Russian River. At the next intersection continue right to stay on Alexander Valley Road. This road runs into Healdsburg Avenue. At the stop sign bear left and continue south on Healdsburg Avenue to the town of Healdsburg.

**Alternate route:** This route out of Cloverdale is less desirable because of having to ride a stretch on Highway 101, though it is not actually a freeway at this point so bikes are permitted. Take Highway 101 out of Cloverdale. Get off at Dutcher Creek and go west. Turn left onto Dry Creek, which is in a beautiful valley, full of lush vineyards. Follow Dry Creek Road to Healdsburg Avenue. Turn right onto Healdsburg Avenue and continue south to the town of Healdsburg.

## Healdsburg to Santa Rosa

From Healdsburg you can make several decisions on which route is best for you.

This route is more direct and parallels closer to Highway 101. Continue on Healdsburg Avenue, which will turn left near Highway 101. Cross the bridge over the Russian River and ride past Memorial Beach. Turn right and go under the freeway on Old Redwood Highway.

**Alternate Route:** Westside Road is a longer, but more scenic route, and will take you through some beautiful forested roads. Make a right turn from Healdsburg Avenue onto Westside Road. Follow Westside Road and then take a left onto Wohler Road and cross the Russian River. Take a left again onto River Road and head back toward Old Redwood Highway.

From this point you can choose whether to ride through the downtown section of Santa Rosa or to avoid it and take the back roads on the east side of the freeway.

## Santa Rosa to Petaluma

**West Side Route.** This route parallels the west side of the freeway and avoids downtown Santa Rosa by using the back roads. Old Redwood Highway junction with Mark West Springs Road (River Road). Turn right and follow for about a mile to the first stoplight after the freeway. Turn left onto Fulton Road (heading south). Fulton Road will turn into North Wright Road. Turn left. on College Avenue and go to Stony Point Road turn right and follow Stony Point to Highway 116, which is a very busy road. Turn left on Highway 116 for about a block, then quickly turn right and pick up Stony Point Road again. Continue on Stony Point Road to Petaluma Blvd. North. Turn right onto Petaluma Blvd. North to Skillman Lane and turn right.

**East Side Route.** This route parallels the east side of the freeway and takes you into the heart of downtown Santa Rosa, which may be a preferred route for some. From Old Redwood Highway continue to Santa Rosa and bear left at Mendocino Avenue. Continue along Mendocino Avenue to Santa Rosa Junior College. Turn left onto Pacific Avenue, and then right onto Humboldt. Cross College Avenue. At Fifth Street make a slight jog to the left, then right again onto D Street. Continue to Sonoma Avenue and make a left turn. At Brookwood Avenue turn right. Cross Highway 12 and go past the Sonoma County Fairgrounds. Follow Brookwood as it turns right onto Allan Way. Bear right onto Aston Avenue, and continue past the rows of horse stables. At the stop sign on Petaluma Hill Road turn left.

Continue on Petaluma Hill Road for about 11 miles until you reach the small town of Penngrove. Go through the town to the stop sign at Old Redwood Highway. Turn left onto Old Redwood Highway and follow it for a mile or so. At Ely Road make a left (Caution! This can be a busy intersection). Turn right onto Corona Road and continue over Highway 101 to Petaluma Blvd. North. Cross the boulevard onto Skillman Lane.

At the flashing red light turn left onto Marshall Avenue. Turn right onto Magnolia Avenue and left onto Lohrman Lane. (Caution! There is a blind hill at the intersection.) Turn left onto Bodega Avenue (another busy road). Turn right onto Cleveland Lane, left onto Western Avenue and right at Howard Street (Five Corners), which becomes Sixth Street. Turn left at D Street to get to Walnut Park. From here you can link up with the "Petaluma to the Golden Gate Bridge" ride in *Marin County Bike Trails.*

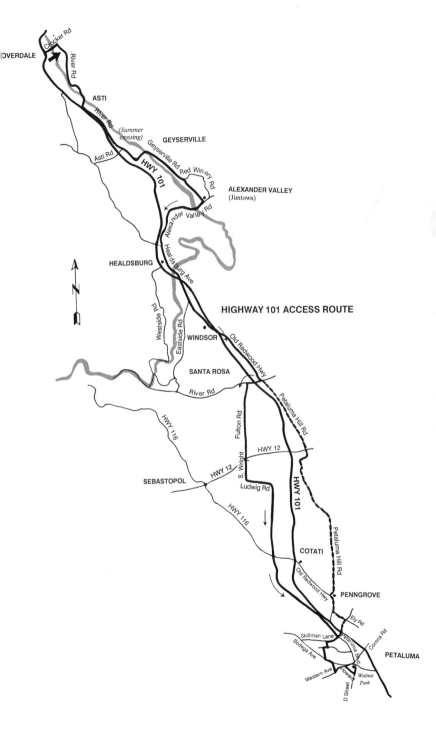

HIGHWAY 101 ACCESS ROUTE

# RIDES BY RATINGS

## EASY RIDES
*(short rides, easy grades, good for beginners and children)*

## MEDIUM RIDES
*(longer rides, some hills, not too strenuous)*

## CHALLENGING RIDES
*(extensive rides with strenuous grades, for more experienced cyclists)*

## MOUNTAIN BIKE RIDES

## HIGHWAY 101 ACCESS ROUTE

# BICYCLE SHOPS IN SONOMA COUNTY

*Analy Bike Shop*
961 Gravenstein Hwy South
Sebastopol, CA 95472
(707) 823-0425

*The Bicycle Factory*
143 Kentucky Street
Petaluma, CA 94952
(707) 763-7515

*Bike Hut*
917 Golf Course Drive,
Rohnert Park, CA 94928
(707) 585-8594

*The Bike Peddler*
1462 Mendocino Avenue
Santa Rosa, CA 95401
(707) 573-0113

*Cloverdale Cyclery*
127 East First Street
Cloverdale, CA 95425
(707) 894-2841

*Cycle Connection*
345 West College Avenue,
Santa Rosa, CA 95401
(707) 578-3999

*Dale's Schwinn Cyclery*
605 College Avenue
Santa Rosa, CA 95404
(707) 528-2400

*Dave's Bike-Sport*
1163 Yulupa Avenue
Santa Rosa, CA 95405
(707) 528-3283

*Goodtime Bicycle Company*
18315 Sonoma Highway
Boyes Hot Springs, CA 95476
(707) 938-0453

*The Hub Cyclery*
70 West Cotati Avenue
Cotati, CA 94928
(707) 795-6670

*Pedal Pusher Bicycle Center*
1599 Cleveland Avenue
Santa Rosa, CA 95401
(707) 528-0461

*Petaluma Schwinn Cyclery*
1080 Petaluma Boulevard North
Petaluma, CA 94952
(707) 762-1990

*Ride-On Bikes*
108 Petaluma Avenue,
Sebastopol, CA 95472
(707) 829-BIKE

*Rincon Cyclery*
4927 Sonoma Hwy
Santa Rosa, CA 95404
(707) 538-0868

*Rohnert Park Cyclery*
205 Southwest Blvd.
Rohnert Park, CA 94928
(707) 664-8706

*Spoke Folk Cyclery*
249 Center Street
Healdsburg, CA 95448
(707) 433-7171

# POINTS OF INTEREST

## Bodega Bay

*Bodega Marine Lab*
*Bay Flat Road at Hwy 1, Bodega Bay*          *(707) 875-3511*

Marine life research laboratories run by the University of California. Tours on Fridays 1:30-4. Open all year.

*Sonoma Coast State Beaches*

From Bodega Head to the Russian River. Activities at this 5,000-acre park include picnicking at Wright's Beach and Rock Point, fishing, camping, hiking, horseback riding and surfing.

*Whale watching.* From December to early February, the California gray whales migrate south to Baja, California to bear their young and to breed in the warm waters. From March to mid-April, they return to the cooler waters of Alaska to feed. The best vista points along the coast are: Timber Cove, Sea Ranch, Bodega Head, Fort Ross and Salt Point.

## Cazadero

*Berry's Saw Mill*
*Cazadero Hwy and Hwy 116, Cazadero*

Watch trees being processed into lumber. Visitors are free to explore the mill informally. Phone ahead to make sure the mill is operating.

## Cloverdale

*Bandiera Winery*
*793 South Cloverdale Blvd., Cloverdale*          *(707) 894-4298*

Tasting and sales. Open daily 10-5.

*Pastori Wines*
*23189 Geyserville Avenue*          *(707) 857-3418*

Pastori Winery has long been a small family winery run by Frank Pastori and his wife, Edith. Open daily 9-5; closed major holidays.

*Pat Paulsen Vineyards*
*26155 Asti Store Road, Cloverdale*          *(707) 894-3197*

Picnic area and adjacent shops. Tasting room in historical Asti Village. Open daily 10-6 except Christmas and New Year's Day.

## Geyserville

*Alexander Valley Fruit & Trading Co.*
*5110 Hwy 128, Geyserville*          *(707) 433-1944*

A country winery with picnic grounds.

*Geyser Peak Winery*
*22281 Redwood Hwy North, Geyserville*     *(707) 433-6585*

Geyserville's first winery. Wines served in tasting room constructed of old redwood tanks and stained glass windows. Picnic areas, hiking trails. Tours by appointment only. Open daily 9-5..

*J. Pedroncelli Vineyards*
*1220 Canyon Road, Geyserville*     *(707) 857-3531*

Bonded in 1904, the original winery and buildings were purchased in 1927 by Giovanni Pedroncelli. Wine-tasting and sales. Tours by appointment only. Open daily 10-5.

*Nervo Winery*
*19550 Old Redwood Hwy South, Geyserville*     *(707) 857-3417*

Established in 1888, Nervo is one of the county's oldest small wineries. Classic example of turn-of-the-century architecture in Sonoma County. Rustic setting, grape arbor, antique winery equipment distplay. Picnic fixin's. Wine-tasting and sales. Open daily 10-5.

*Souverain Cellars*
*Independence Lane (off Hwy 101), Geyserville*     *(707) 433-2001*

Tours, wine-tasting, gift shop, restaurant offers Sunday brunch.

*Trentadue Winery*
*19170 Old Redwood Hwy, Geyserville*     *(707) 433-3104*

A small family winery. Large gift shop and attractive picnic area available. Wine-tasting and sales. Tours by appointment only. Open daily 10-5.

## Glen Ellen

*Glen Ellen Winery*
*1883 London Ranch Road, Glen Ellen*     *(707) 996-1066*

Established in 1868. Wine-tasting and sales. Tours on weekends. Open daily 9-4:30.

*Jack London State Historic Park*
*Jack London Ranch Road (near Hwy 12), Glen Ellen*

Former the home of writer, Jack London, this beautiful 800-acre park has miles of rolling hills. The House of Happy Walls was built by Mrs. London in 1919 shortly after her husband's death. It stores the collection of South Pacific artifacts, part of London's 18,000-volume library and many of the original furnishing and memorabilia of his life and travels. "The Wolf House" was destroyed by fire in 1913 before the Londons could move in. Only the walls and chimney made of volcanic stone remain. London's grave is nearby, marked by a large boulder.

*The World of Jack London*
*14300 Arnold Drive (near Hill Road), Glen Ellen*     *(707) 996-2888*

This museum, located in the Jack London Book Store, features rare and unusual memorabilia of the California author. Russ Kingman, author of A Pictorial Life of Jack London, offers a slide show and filmstrips.

*Valley of the Moon Winery*
*777 Madrone Road, Glen Ellen*                    *(707) 996-6941*

Family-owned and operated since 1941. Wine-tasting and sales. Picnic area. Open daily 9-5.

## Guerneville

*Armstrong Redwood State Reserve*
*Armstrong Woods Road (off Hwy 116), Guerneville*

This 752-acre park is home to Sonoma County's oldest and loveliest redwoods. There are picnic areas and walking and hiking trails.

*Austin Creek State Recreation Area*
*17000 Armstrong Woods Road, Guerneville*

Fish, camp, ride horseback or hike at this expansive 4,236-acre park. The Redwood Lake Campground, a rustic area with primitive campsites, is a 4 to 5-mile hike from the main road.

*F. Korbel and Bros.*
*13250 River Road, Guerneville*                    *(707) 887-2294*

World-famous Korbel Champagne Cellars. Elegant tasting room, tours every 45 minutes 9:30-4. Picnic area. Open daily 9-5.

*Quicksilver Mine Company*
*14028 Armstrong Woods Road, Guerneville*           *(707) 869-9357*

Country store specializing in products made, grown or created in Sonoma County. Includes art gallery. Open daily 11-5:30.

## Healdsburg

*Healdsburg Memorial Beach Park*
*Healdsburg Avenue, near Front Street, Healdsburg*

This popular park features a beach with lifeguards two diving boards and a boat launching pad, snack bars and a picnic area. Restrooms are available.

*Lake Sonoma and Warm Springs Dam*
*Dry Creek Road (at Rockpile Road), Healdsburg*

This 319-foot-high Warm Springs Dam is the largest structure ever built in Sonoma County designed to control Russian River flooding. The visitors' center have exhibits about the dam and the history of the region.

*Congressman Don Clausen Fish Hatchery*
*Dry Creek Road, Healdsburg*

Built to protect the migrating silver salmon and steelhead trout because of the construction of the Dry Creek Dam. It also raises king salmon. The hatchery is operated by the California Department of Fish and Game.

*Alexander Valley Vineyards*
*8644 Hwy 128, Healdsburg*                          *(707) 433-7209*

The vineyard and winery are located on the original homestead of Cyrus Alexander, dating from the 1840s. Tasting 10-5.

*Belvedere Winery*
*4035 Westside Road, Healdsburg*                    *(800) 292-9463*

Tasting and sales Monday through Saturday. Tours by appointment only. Picnic area. Open daily 9-5.

*Clos Du Bois*
*5 Fitch Street, Healdsburg*                         *(707) 433-5576*

Wine-tasting and sales . Tours by appointment only. Open daily 10-5.

*Davis Bynum Winery*
*8075 Westside Road*                                 *(707) 433-5852*

Set in a country atmosphere of lush vineyards and hills along Westside Road. Wine-tasting and sales. Picnic grounds. Open daily 10-5.

*Dry Creek Vineyard*
*37770 Lambert Bridge Road, Healdsburg*             *(707) 433-1000*

Built in the 1840's, the winery was the original home of Cyrus Alexander. Friendly, informal atmosphere and pleasant picnic grounds. Tours by appointment only. Open daily 10:30-4:30.

*Field Stone Winery*
*10075 Hwy 128, Healdsburg*                          *(707) 433-7266*

Beautiful picnic area, summer evening concerts. Wine-tasting and sales. Open daily 10-5.

*Foppiano Vineyards*
*12707 Old Redwood Hwy, Healdsburg*                  *(707) 433-7272*

Founded in 1896, this winery has the longest history of family ownership and operation in Sonoma County. Wine-tasting and sales. Tours by appointment only. Open daily 10-4:30.

*Hop Kiln Winery*
*6050 Westside Road, Healdsburg*                     *(707) 433-6491*

Restored in 1905 this winery is set on 240 acres. It is a state historic landmark and the site of several movies. Historic tasting room in landmark hops barn and picnic area. Open daily 10-5.

*Johnson's Alexander Valley Wines*
*8329 State Hwy 128, Healdsburg*                     *(707) 433-2319*

Built in the 1930's. Open house and concerts once a month. Occasional theater pipe organ concerts. Picnic tables. Wine-tasting and sales. Open daily 10-5.

*Lambert Bridge Winery*
*4085 West Dry Creek Road, Healdsburg*              *(707) 433-5855*

Tasting and sales open daily 10-4:30.

*Lytton Springs Winery*
*640 Lytton Springs Road, Healdsburg*               *(707) 433-7721*

Wine-tasting and sales. Tours by appointment only. Open daily 9-5.

*Mazzocco Vineyards, Inc.*
*1400 Lytton Springs Road, Healdsburg*                    *(707) 433-9035*
Open daily 10-4.

*Mill Creek Vineyards*
*1401 Westside Road, Healdsburg*                          *(707) 433-5098*
Picnic area. Wine-tasting and sales. Open daily 10-4:30.

*Preston Vineyards*
*9282 West Dry Creek Road, Healdsburg*                    *(707) 433-3372*
Retail sales Monday through Friday 11:00-3:00.

*Robert Stemmler Winery*
*3805 Lambert Bridge Road, Healdsburg*                    *(707) 433-6334*
Founded in 1977. Picnicking by reservation. Tasting and retail sales 10:30-4:30 daily.

*Sausal Winery*
*7370 Highway 128, Healdsburg*                            *(707) 433-2285*
Alexander Valley's oldest winemaking family. Tasting room open daily 10-4. Tours by appointment only.

*Simi Winery*
*16275 Healdsburg Avenue, Healdsburg*                     *(707) 433-6981*
Founded over a century ago. Picnic area. Wine-tasting and sales. Tours at 11:00, 1:00, 3:00. Opendaily 10-4:30.

*Soda Rock Winery*
*8015 Highway 128 (Alexander Valley), Healdsburg*         *(707) 433-1830*
Established in the 1880's, Soda Rock Winery has played an important role in the history of Alexander Valley. The Tomka family, Hungarian immigrants, invite visitors to taste wines among the old casks, or to picnic in a garden setting. Open daily 10-5.

*William Wheeler Winery*
*130 Plaza Street, Healdsburg*                            *(707) 433-8786*
Located in downtown Healdsburg. Tasting and sales open 10-4. Thursday through Monday.

## Kenwood

*Morton's Warm Spring Recreation Park*
*1651 Warm Springs Road, Kenwood*                         *(707) 833-5511*
The park has two swimming pools, a wading pool, a softball field, horseshoe pits, a volleyball court, snack bar and picnic area with barbecue pits. Open daily May through September, 9-6. Closed during the winter.

*Sugarloaf Ridge State Park*
*2605 Adobe Canyon Road (near Hwy 12), Kenwood*

Popular activities at this 2,373-acre park include camping, picnicking, hiking and horse-back riding. A lodge provides food and drinks and a place to relax.

*Chateau St. Jean Vineyards*
*8555 Sonoma Highway, Kenwood*                          *(707) 833-4134*

Self-guided tour of the fermentation cellar and crush area. Picnic grounds. Wine-tasting and sales. Open daily 10:30-4.

*Kenwood Vineyards*
*9592 Sonoma Hwy, Kenwood*                               *(707) 833-5891*

Rustic tasting room. Tours by appointment only. Open daily 10-4:30.

*Smothers Tasting Room*
*9575 Highway 12, Kenwood*                               *(707) 833-1010*

Owned and operated by the famous Smothers Brothers comedy team. Tasting room housed in rustic cabin.

*St. Francis Vineyards*
*8450 Sonoma Highway, Kenwood*                          *(707) 833-4666*

Picnic area. Wine-tasting and sales. Open daily 10-4:30.

## Penngrove

*Eagle Ridge Winery*
*111 Goodwin Avenue, Penngrove*                          *(707) 664-WINE*

Historic landmark, tasting room, tours, picnic area Open daily 11-4.

## Petaluma

*The Creamery Store*
*711 Western Avenue (at Baker), Petaluma*               *(707) 778-1234*

Petaluma cheeses, gifts, picnic area. Tour of cheese plant, slide show from 10:30. Open Monday through Friday 10-6; Saturday 10-5.

*Marin French Cheese Company*
*7500 Red Hill Road*                                     *(707) 762-6001*

Manufacturer of French cheeses — Camembert, Brie, Breakfast and Schloss. 15-minute tours of the cheese plant from 10-4. Picnic area, lagoon with piped-in background classical music, and picnic supplies. Open daily 9-5.

*Petaluma Adobe Historic State Park*
*3325 Adobe Road (at Casa Grande Road)*                 *(707) 762-4871*

Explore General Mariano Vallejo's Petaluma Rancho, built in 1840 and now open as a museum. Outdoor displays include cowhide racks, the old forge and large ovens where bread was baked for the Rancho inhabitants.

*Petaluma Historic Museum and Library*
*20 Fouth Street (at B Stree), Petaluma*                *(707) 778-4398*

Open Thursday through Monday 1-4.

# Santa Rosa

*Annadel State Park*
*6201 Channel Drive (off Montgomery Drive), Santa Rosa*

This 4,913-acre park features hiking, biking and horseback riding trails, nature walks and exhibits. Visitors can fish at Lake Ilsanjo, and Ledsen Marsh offers wildlife viewing.

*Crane & Sons Melons*
*4947 Petaluma Hill Road, Santa Rosa*                    *(707) 584-5141*

Home of original Crane melons. In season first of September. Tomatoes, corn squash in season. Open daily 10-6, from August 15– November 15.

*Hood Mountain Regional Park*
*3000 Los Alamos Drive (east from Hwy 12), Santa Rosa*

This 1,450-acre park has lovely vistas from the top of the steep trail, as well as on the way up.

*Howarth Memorial Park*
*Summerfield Road (near Montgomery Drive), Santa Rosa*

This 152-acre park offers boat rentals, six tennis courts, a softball field, picnic and barbecue areas, a large playground as well as bicycle, horse and jogging trails. There is a petting zoo, and visitors can feed the ducks at Lake Ralphine.

*Luther Burbank Memorial Gardens*
*204 Santa Rosa Avenue (and Sonoma Avenue), Santa Rosa*

In his 53-years residence in Santa Rosa Luther Burbank developed over 300 plant varieties, including more than 25 marketable vegetables and over 250 varieties of fruits. This national Historical Landmark features experimental gardens once used by the "Plant Wizard," as well as his home with its reflecting pool and green house.

*Matanzas Creek Winery*
*6097 Bennett Valley Road, Santa Rosa*                    *(707) 542-8242*

Wine-tasting and sales. Tours by appointment only.

*Petrified Forest*
*4100 Petrified Forest Road, Calistoga*                    *(707) 942-6667*

Open since 1870. Several ancient petrified trees, many over 100 feet tall, have been unearthed here for display. Covered by volcanic ash when Mt. St. Helena erupted 6 million years ago, the trees are now in unusual formations and colors. Petrified sea shells, clams and marine life can be seen here as well. Museum, picnic grounds, gift shop.

*Ripley's Memorial Museum*
*492 Sonoma Avenue and Santa Rosa Avenue, Santa Rosa*

Dedicated to the unusual and incredible, the museum is housed in a strange and beautiful church built from the planks and boards of a single giant redwood tree. Closed from December to February.

*Sonoma County Museum*
*425 7th Street and B Street, Santa Rosa*

Artifacts and displays documenting the cultural history of Sonoma county and Northern California are exhibited here.

*Spring Lake County Park*
*Newanga Avenue and Summerfield Road*

Popular activities at this 320-acre park include non-motorized boating, swimming, fishing, camping, and picnicking.

## Sebastopol

*Ragle Ranch Park*
*Ragle Road (off Bodega Hwy), Sebastopol*

This 156-acre day-use park, once the Ragle family ranch and still family-owned, offers hiking, biking and equestrian trails.

*Pet-A-Llama Ranch*
*5505 Lone Pine Road, Sebastopol*　　　　　　　　*(707) 823-9395*

Llamas in pasture, woven goods.

## Sonoma

*Buena Vista Winery*
*18000 Old Winery Road, Sonoma*　　　　　　　*(707) 938-1266*

Wine-tasting and sales in historic Press House. Self-guided tours of wine caves. Oldest premium winery in California, built in 1857. State Historic Landmark. Art gallery. Large picnic area. Open daily 10-5.

*Depot Park Historical Museum*
*285 West First Street*　　　　　　　　　　　　*(707) 938-5389*

Open Wednesday through Sundays 1-4 p.m.

*Gundlach-Bundschu Winery*
*3775 Thornsberry Road, Sonoma*　　　　　　　*(707) 938-5277*

Award-winning picturesque winery. Only U.S. producer of Kleinberger. Self-guided tour. Picnic hill with great views. Nature hike. Wine-tasting and sales. Open daily 11-4:30.

*Hacienda Wine Cellars*
*1000 Vineyard Lane, Sonoma*　　　　　　　　　*(707) 938-3220*

Wine garden for picnics overlooking vineyard and pond. Tours by appointment only. Wine-tasting and sales, open daily 10-5.

*Sebastiani Vineyards*
*389 4th Street East, Sonoma*　　　　　　　　　*(707) 938-5532*

Extensive Indian artifact collection and largest collection of hand-carved casks in California. Guided tours. Wine-tasting and sales, open daily 10-5.

*Sonoma Cheese Factory*
*2 Spain Street (on the Plaza), Sonoma*                              *996-1931*

Home of Sonoma Jack Cheese. Large deli, wines, picnic items, outdoor eating, factory viewing, slide presentation on cheese-making and samples. Open daily 9-6.

*Sonoma State Historic Park*
*3rd Street West at Spain Street (on the Plaza)*

Once the northernmost town of the Mexican empire, Sonoma boasts a number of historically significant structures: the Blue Wing Inn, the Swiss Hotel, the sites of General Vallejo's two Sonoma homes, and Mission San Francisco Solano de Sonoma. Admission 50 cents. Open daily 9-5.

*Stornetta's Dairy*
*4300 Fremont Drive, Sonoma*                              *(707) 938-7354*

Watch cows being milked. Taped recording that explains milking process. Open daily 2-4.

*Train Town*
*20264 Broadway Avenue, Sonoma*                              *(707) 938-3912*

Ten-acre railroad park. 15-minute train trip; refreshments. Steam trains travel through 10 acres of landscaped park filled with trees, lakes, bridges, tunnels and reconstructed historic structures. Open 10:30-5:30 weekends and holidays; daily June through Labor Day.

*Vella Cheese Company*
*315 2nd Street East, Sonoma*                              *(707) 938-3232*

Visitors are welcome to observe the cheese-making process on days of production. Open Monday through Saturday 9-6; Sunday 10-5.

## Windsor

*Piper Sonoma Cellars*
*11447 Old Redwood Highway, Windsor*                              *(707) 433-8843*

Tours and tasting April-December, 10-5. Light lunches by reservation only.

*Rodney Strong Vineyards/Windsor Vineyard*
*11455 Old Redwood Highway, Windsor*                              *(707) 433-6511*

Visitors are served wines at their table by friendly and knowledgeable staff. Unique architecture. Winery features concerts and cultural events during the summer. Hourly tours. Picnic in Greek theater. Open daily 10-5.

*Windsor Waterworks and Slides*
*8225 Conde Lane (near Old Redwood Hwy), Windsor*

Slide and splash at this water park which features "The Doom Flume" and other water slides. There is also a swimming pool, wading pool, game room, snack bar and picnic area.

# CALIFORNIA BICYCLE LAWS

The following are excerpts taken from the 1987 California Vehicle Code relating to the operation and equipping of bicycles. Some of the sections of the laws listed have been reworded slightly and/or abbreviated.

## RIGHTS AND RESPONSIBILITIES                     21200

A. Every person riding a bicycle upon a highway has all the rights and is subject to all the provisions applicable to the driver of a motor vehicle, including stopping at stop signs, traveling in the same direction as motorists, granting right-of-way to pedestrians and vehicles, and obeying traffic signals.

B. *Riding Under the Influence of Alcohol or Drugs*          *21200.5*
It is unlawful for any person to ride a bicycle upon a highway while under the influence of an alcoholic beverage or any drug, or under the combined influence of an alcoholic beverage and any drug. A conviction of a violation shall be punished by a fine of not more than two hundred fifty dollars ($250).

## EQUIPMENT REQUIREMENTS                          21201

A. *Brakes* — No person shall operate a bicycle on a roadway unless it is equipped with a brake which will enable the operator to make one braked wheel skid on dry, level, clean pavement.

B. *Handlebars* — No person shall operate on the highway any bicycle equipped with handlebars so raised that the operator must elevate his hands above the level of his shoulders in order to grasp the normal steering grip area.

C. *Bicycle Size* — No person shall operate upon any highway a bicycle which is of such a size as to prevent the operator from safely stopping the bicycle, supporting it in an upright position with at least one foot on the ground, and restarting it in a safe manner.

D. *Lights and Reflectors* — Every bicycle operated upon any highway during darkness shall be equipped with:

   1. a lamp emitting a white light which, while the bicycle is in motion, illuminates the highway in front of the bicyclist and is visible from a distance of 300 feet in front and from the sides of the bicycle.

   2. a red reflector visible from a distance of 500 feet to the rear.

   3. a white or yellow reflector mounted on each pedal visible from the front and rear of the bicycle from a distance of 200 feet.

   4. a white or yellow reflector on each side forward of the center of the bicycle, and a white or red reflector on each side to the rear of the center of the bicycle, except that bicycles which are equipped with reflectorized tires on the front and rear need not be equipped with these side reflectors.

## OPERATION ON ROADWAY 21202

A. *Two-way Street* — Any person operating a bicycle upon a roadway at a speed less than the normal speed of traffic moving in the same direction at such time shall ride as close as practicable to the right-hand curb or edge of the roadway except:

1. when overtaking and passing another bicycle or motor vehicle proceeding in the same direction.

2. when preparing for a left turn at an intersection or into a private road or driveway.

3. when reasonably necessary to avoid conditions (including, but not limited to, fixed or moving objects, vehicles, bicycles, pedestrians, animals, surface hazards, or substandard width lanes) that make it unsafe to continue along the right-hand curb or edge.

B. *One-Way Street* — Any person operating a bicycle upon a roadway, which carries traffic in one direction only has two or more marked traffic lanes may ride as near the left-hand curb or edge of such roadway as practicable; however, this is the only situation in which you may do so.

## HITCHING RIDES 21203

No person riding upon a bicycle shall attach the bicycle or himself to any streetcar or vehicle on the roadway.

## RIDING ON BICYCLE 21204

A. No person operating a bicycle upon a highway shall ride other than upon or astride a permanent and regular attached seat.

B. No operator shall allow a person riding as a passenger, and no person shall ride as a passenger, on a bicycle upon a highway other than upon or astride a separate attached seat. If the passenger is four years of age or younger, or weighs 40 pounds or less, the seat shall have adequate provision for retaining the passenger in place and for protecting the passenger from moving parts of the bicycle.

C. No person operating a bicycle upon a highway shall allow any person who is four years of age or younger, or weighs 40 pounds or less, to ride as a passenger on a bicycle unless that passenger is wearing a helmet meeting the standards of the American National Standards Institute (ANSI Z 90.4 bicycle helmet standards) or of the Snell Memorial Foundation's 1984 Standard for Protective Headgear for Use in Bicycling.

D. Wearing a helmet means having a helmet of good fit fastened securely upon the head with the helmet straps.

## CARRYING ARTICLES 21205

No person operating a bicycle shall carry any package, bundle, or article which prevents the operator from keeping at least one hand upon the handlebars.

## BICYCLE LANES 21208

A. Whenever a bicycle lane has been established on a roadway, any person operating a bicycle upon the roadway at a speed less than the normal speed of traffic moving in the same direction shall ride within the bicycle lane, except:

   1. when overtaking and passing another bicycle, vehicle, or pedestrian within the lane or about to enter the lane if such overtaking and passing cannot be done safely within the lane.

   2. when preparing for a left turn at an intersection or into a private road or driveway.

   3. when reasonably necessary to leave the bicycle lane to avoid debris or other hazardous conditions.

B. No person operating a bicycle shall leave a bicycle lane until the movement can be made with reasonable safety and then only after giving an appropriate signal in the event that any vehicle may be affected by the movement.

## BICYCLE PARKING 21210

No person shall leave a bicycle lying on its side on any sidewalk, or shall park a bicycle on a sidewalk in any other position, so that there is not an adequate path for pedestrian traffic.

## FREEWAYS 21960

A. The Department of Transportation and local authorities may prohibit or restrict the use of the freeways or any portion thereof by pedestrians, bicycles or other nonmotorized traffic or by any person operating a motor-driven cycle or a motorized bicycle.

B. Such prohibitory regulation shall be effective when appropriate signs giving notice thereof are erected upon any freeway and the approaches thereto.

## HAND SIGNALS 22111

All required signals given by hand and arm shall be given in the following manner:

*Left Turn* — hand and arm extended horizontally beyond the left side of the bicycle.

*Right Turn* — hand and arm extended upward beyond the left side of the bicycle, or right hand and arm extended horizontally to the right side of the bicycle [not recommended].

*Stop or sudden decrease of speed* — hand and arm extended downward beyond the left side of the bicycle.

# BICYCLING TIPS

With the emphasis on fitness and exercise bicycling has once again taken off as one of the enjoyable sports of all time. Understanding your bicycle and its limitations are essential in preparing yourself for an enjoyable outing.

## GENERAL RULES OF THE ROAD

1. *Keep to the right and move with the flow of traffic.* Riding on the left against traffic increases the chance for accidents because the force of collision is greater. Riding the wrong way is a leading cause of accidents between bicycle and motorist. Only pedestrians are permitted to travel facing oncoming traffic.

2. *Ride in single file off to the right side of the road.*

3. *Signal your moves so that motorists know what you intend to do.* Use the correct hand signals (see California Bicycle Laws).

4. *Never ride on freeways, toll roads, or major highways.* At those high speeds you could become severely injured or killed. Highway shoulders are frequently littered with broken glass and other hazardous debris. Avoid congested streets and use bike paths and lanes wherever possible.

5. *Watch out for soft or uneven shoulders and other road surface hazards.* You could easily skid and slip out into the road. When riding on dirt roads be very careful and slow down before turning corners. You could skid on sandy or gravel surfaces.

6. *Cross railroad tracks at a right angle (head-on).* When they are wet, walk your bicycle across them.

7. *Avoid riding in the rain.* Wet brakes and pavement can more than double your stopping distance and can cause a serious skid as well. The slippery surface and impaired visibility make riding in the rain a real hazard. Dry out your brakes after going through water by braking slightly for a short distance.

8. *Don't ride at night without headlights, taillights and reflectors on your bike* (see California Bicycle Laws). Also, wear reflectorized tape on your clothes or wear a reflective vest or jacket.

9. *Watch out for child cyclists.* Children on bicycles tend to weave from side to side, turn unpredictably without signaling, and may even collide with you when you are trying to pass them.

10. *In general, drive your bicycle defensively! Watch out for the other guy! Know your right of way, but don't insist upon it.* Remember that motorists often do not see bicycles, or even remember to watch out for them. Leave yourself enough room to take quick defensive action.

## Bicycling in the City

1. *When traveling straight keep to the right.* Look behind to check on traffic more frequently.

2. *Don't do anything unpredictable,* like stopping suddenly, without having made sure nobody is following so closely as to be endangered.

3. *Keep your hands on or near the brake levers at all times* so that you can stop instantly if you have to. Keep your toe straps loose.

4. *Never ride on sidewalks unless special signs indicate that bicycles are permitted.*

5. *Watch out for doors of parked cars opening ahead of you, or for cars pulling out into traffic.* Motorists forget to watch for bicycles, so cyclists had better watch out for them.

6. *Be extremely careful at intersections.* That's where most accidents happen. Watch out for cars making a turn across your path. If traffic is heavy, walk your bike with pedestrian traffic; use the crosswalks.

7. *Leave enough room for others to overtake you whenever possible without endangering yourself.*

8. *Watch out for potholes and driveway curbs.* Touring bike wheels are very delicate and you may damage your tire or rim if you hit one. You may also wind up on the ground. You can avoid some damage to your bike by raising yourself off the saddle momentarily, if the hole or curb cannot be avoided.

9. *Watch out for drainage grates.* Those facing your direction can catch your wheel, forcing it into an abrupt stop and sending you flying over the handlebars.

10. *Don't turn left without first having made sure the road is clear behind you,* giving a clear signal and moving over to the center of the road (or to a left-turn lane) well ahead of your actual turn.

11. *Watch for approaching road users coming the other way and crossing or turning traffic coming from side roads.* Ride far enough out into the road to keep an eye out for crossing traffic. Look well ahead, and scan the edge of the road for clues to the unexpected, such as car doors opening, pedestrians stepping out, cars ahead of you turning off or pulling up.

12. *In general, look ahead, think ahead, and use the skill you developed as a motorist, so you will be safe as a bicyclist too.*

## Bicycle Touring

1. *When touring long distances, both you and your bicycle should be in good condition.*

2. *Carry spare parts with you,* such as simple repair tools, a patch kit or spare tube, and a bicycle pump.

3. *Never begin a trip on an empty stomach.* Eat *before* becoming hungry; drink *before* becoming thirsty. Take a water bottle with you. Carry

some quick energy foods, such as a candy bar or fruit to snap you back and supply you with renewed energy. A banana will not only fill you up but is an excellent source of potassium.

4. *Stay in single file when riding with others.* Wait for the slower ones to catch up.

5. *Don't follow too closely behind.* You may not be able to avoid a pot-hole, obstacle, or a fallen cyclist in time. Be sure that you can see far enough ahead to brake safely.

## Off-Road Bicycling

Off-road bicycling has become a challenging, new sport where bicycles are now riding on dirt roads and rugged terrain once only accessible to hikers and equestrians.

1. *Wear a helmet at all times as well as protective clothing, including eye protection and biking gloves.*

2. *Carry with you sufficient drinking water, a tire pump, a spare tub or patch kit, tire irons, special tools and an adjustable wrench.*

3. *Have an understanding of your personal ability and equipment, and prepared for the unexpected.* Your needs will differ, depending on where you ride and the type of riding you do. Be prepared and equipped to look after yourself and your bike.

4. *Plan ahead.* Each ride should be determined by your ability and equipment, the terrain and weather conditions.

5. *If you ride alone,* leave word with someone regarding where you plan to go, your route and anticipated time of return.

6. *Look ahead and anticipate any hazards in your path.* Evaluate the road or trail surface ahead of you, to pick out in advance the kind of obstacles that will be likely to stop your front wheel — deep chuckholes and high ridges, ditches, trees, logs and large rocks.

7. *Try to anticipate where somebody or something might appear suddenly,* such as pedestrians, cyclists, motorists, children or animals. Also, consider the liability factor involved in any impact you may have on them.

8. *Before starting out, check your seat height and your tire pressure.* Experiment with both. A quick-relase seat bolt will allow you to adjust your seat height easily on the trail. You can tailor it as you go.

9. *Don't over-inflate your tires.* You will lose traction. Most off-road tires have a suggested high and low tire pressure marked on the side For off-road bicycling, use the lower suggested pressure.

10. *When riding down hills lower your seat a little.* This will lower your center of gravity and keep your seat out of your way so that you can stand up and shift your body weight forward and backward over each bump.

11. *Maintain a comfortable steady pace, increasing your speed slightly as you climb a hill.* Select a comfortable gear and then gear down one; you can always gear up, if necessary.

## Off-Road Riding in Sonoma County Parks

When using the Sonoma County Park System it is important to know the park regulations for bicycles. Check with a ranger or other official regarding the current status of bicycle regulations on the land you plan to ride.

1. *Stay on designated bike trails.* Bicycles are not permitted on many hiking trails. *There is a fine for violating this regulation.*

2. *Avoid practices that contribute to erosion.* Avoid muddy sections, excessive braking or skidding and cross-country routes. Don't trample native vegetation.

3. *Don't disturb wildlife.* Give them time to move away from your path.

4. *Pack out litter.* If you have room, pack out more than your share.

5. *Slow down and pass with care.* The maximum speed for all vehicles is 15 miles per hour. At blind turns and when passing others 5 miles per hour is required.

6. *Slow your speed and anticipate switchbacks and curves cautiously.* A hiker or horse may be approaching just around the bend.

7. *Be careful not to startle or interfere with hikers or horses on the trail.* Pass with care by letting others know of your presence well in advance by ringing a handlebar bell or with a greeting, "On your left (or right)."

8. *Always yield to hikers and equestrians.* If necessary, dismount your bicycle and wait for them to pass or signal you to pass. Be especially careful when approaching a horse. A skittish one may shy at an unfamiliar object, such as a bicycle, and kick out or run away, endangering its rider and/or anyone in its path.

9. Abide by the code of the responsible off-road bicyclist: *Take only pictures; leave only knobby prints.*

## CLOTHING

1. *Always wear a bicycle helmet* to minimize the effects of a possible head injury in case of a bicycle traffic accident or just falling off your bike. About 50-75 percent of all bicycling fatalities can be directly attributed to head injury. Bicycling helmets provide a cushioning effect in a fall. Make sure that your helmet is especially designed for biking and meets the ANSI Z90.4 or Snell standards.

2. *Clothing worn on any bicycle trip should be brightly colored* (suggested colors are yellow, orange, and white). To make sure you can be seen in the dark, wear reflective tape on your clothes, or wear a reflective vest or jacket. Don't wear loose clothes that can get caught in the pedals or wheels.

3. *Biking clothes are usually made of polypropelene or Lycra and are aeronomically designed to reduce wind resistance.*

   • Shorts provide maximum comfort in warm weather. In cooler weather long cycling tights are comfortable and safe to wear. Not only are they padded, but, because they stretch they won't restrict your movements.

   • Jackets are designed to protect you from wind reistance in front but are ventilated in back against heat build-up.

   • Jerseys are made of fabric that keeps you warm against sweat and can breathe. They also provide deep back pockets for snacks and money.

4. *When wearing long pants wear a leg clip or band on your right leg* (preferable wear one on each leg) to keep the pants away from the chain. Also consider wearing biking underwear under regular pants.

5. *Wear shoes at all times* to avoid getting your toes caught in moving parts. Biking shoes are made stiffer to give you better support than standard shoes and are more efficient.

6. *Wear biking gloves on long rides.* The padding will protect your hands from constant pressure to the palms, which might cause temporary nerve damage and will also protect your hands if you fall. Without padding to protect your palms your hands will become numb and could eventually contract carpal tunnel syndrome. To prevent this shift your hand position often and keep your elbows bent and shoulders relaxed.

## BICYCLE EQUIPMENT

1. *Make sure that your bicycle is the right size for you.* One that is too large or too small will be more difficult to control and uncomfortable to ride. To measure your bike, straddle the top tube of the frame with both feet flat on the ground. You should have 1 to 2 inches of clearance and be able to mount and dismount easily.

2. *Adjust the saddle to the correct height.* A saddle that is placed too low can cause fatigue and discomfort, and can considerably reduce your riding efficiency. Raise the saddle until your bare heel, placed on the pedal in its lowest position, is almost fully extended without your knees locking in place.

3. *Toe clips are highly recommended* because they let your muscles pull up as well push down on the pedals. Keep them loose when you're just learning to use them and when you're riding on city streets.

### Shifting

1. *Understand your gear shift controls.* Shifting into the wrong gear can not only wear parts, but can also make you lose control of your bicycle (see following page).

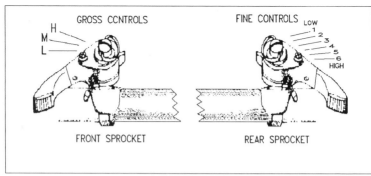

*Gear Shift Levers (18 speeds)*

2. *Shift when pedaling becomes too difficult or too easy.* Try to maintain a steady pace.

3. *When making any gear changes keep the pedals moving.* Never change gears when not in motion.

4. *Avoid cross-chaining your gears* (using the small front chain ring and small rear sprocket, and large front chain ring and large back chain ring) This is especially bad with triple front chain rings which are common on mountain bikes. They put stress on the derailleur and tend to stretch the chain.

5. *Shift to a lower gear <u>before</u> you reach an upgrade.* Otherwise you will put too much strain on the gears and the chain.

6. *The gear-shift levers* should be moved slowly, until a solid "clicking" sound is heard. Any chattering or scraping sounds can be cleared by slight lever movement. Newer bikes have "index" shifters which make shifting much easier.

7. *When approaching a stop, move your left gear shift lever to the low range.* That way you don't have to pedal so hard when you first start up.

## Braking

1. *When braking on the straight-away, use the rear brake first, followed by the front brake.* Exception: in loose gravel or on a slippery surface, use only the rear brake. Avoid using the front brake alone. It can send you flying over the handlebars.

2. *When braking in an emergency situation, shift your body weight toward the rear of the bicycle.*

## Bicycle Maintenance

1. *Drive a safe bicycle. Make sure it is in good mechanical condition.* Oil squeaks and moving parts, adjust gears and brakes, check tire pressure, and tighten nuts and bolts periodically.

2. *Never back up your bike or pedal backwards.* Derailleurs are not designed for going backwards and may become damaged.

3. *Never sit on your bicycle with the kickstand down.* You can put considerable stress on the frame and damage it.

4. *Avoid getting water or sand into the rear wheel.* It can damage the gears, chain and bearings. If you do get sand on your bicycle be sure to wash it off at the earliest opportunity.

5. *Keep your tires at full pressure.* Use a bicycle tire pump. Service station pumps use 185 pounds of pressure and may inflate your tire too fast with too much pressure, and could cause a blowout. Their gauges may also be inaccurate. If you must use a service station pump, inflate your tire in short spurts and carry your own pressure gauge. (You might consider equipping your bike with heavy-duty inner tubes or tire protectors to help avoid flats.)

6. *Always lock your bicycle when it is going to be left unattended for any length of time.* Use a strong, case-hardened steel chain or cable and heavy-duty lock. Kryptonite locks, though bulky, are virtually theft-proof. Secure the chain through both wheels *and* frame, not just through the wheel, and then around a stationary object, such as a bike rack, tree or post.

7. *Store your bicycle with both gear shift levers in such a position as to leave the cables relaxed.*

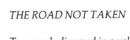

## THE ROAD NOT TAKEN

Two roads diverged in a yellow wood
And sorry I could not travel both
And be one traveler, long I stood
And looked down one as far as I coul
to where it bent in the undergrowth;

Then took the other, as just as fair,
And having perhaps the better claim,
Because it was grassy and wanted wea
Though as for that, the passing there
Had worn them really about the sam

And both that morning equally lay
In leaves no step had trodden black.
Oh, I kept the first for another day!
Yet knowing how way leads on to wa
I doubted if I should ever come back.

I shall be telling this with a sigh
Somewhere ages and ages hence:
Two roads diverged in a wood, and I
I took the one less traveled by,
And that has made all the difference.
ROBERT FROST